BTEC First
Sport

STUDY GUIDE

A PEARSON COMPANY

BTEC First Study Guide: Sport

Published by:
Edexcel Limited
One90 High Holborn
London WC1V 7BH
www.edexcel.org.uk

Distributed by:
Pearson Education Limited
Edinburgh Gate
Harlow
Essex CM20 2JE

First published 2007

Eighth Impression 2009

ISBN 978-1-84690-177-5

Project managed, designed and typeset by Bookcraft Ltd, Stroud, Gloucestershire
Printed by Ashford Colour Press Ltd, Gosport

Cover image © Brand X Pictures/Alamy

The Publisher's policy is to use paper manufactured from sustainable forests.

All reasonable efforts have been made to trace and contact original copyright owners.

Contents

Preface

Following a BTEC programme is an exciting way to study. It gives you the opportunity to develop the knowledge, skills and understanding that you will need in the world of work.

BTECs are very different from GCSEs; a BTEC puts *you* in charge of your own learning. This guide has been written specially for you, to help you get started and succeed on your BTEC First course.

The **introduction**, Your BTEC First, tells you about your new course. This will be your companion through the BTEC First, as it:

- tells you how your BTEC will differ from GCSE;

- suggests how you can plan your time;

- explains ways to make the most of visits, guest speakers and work experience;

- advises you about resources and how to find information;

- gives you advice on making presentations and doing assignments.

The **activities** give you tasks to do on your own, in small groups or as a class. You will have the opportunity to put into practice the theory you learn. The activities will help you prepare for assessment by practising your skills and showing you how much you know. These activities are *not* intended for assessment.

The sample **marked assignments** (also sometimes called marked assessments) show you what other students have done to gain a Pass, Merit or Distinction. By seeing what past students have done, you should be able to improve your own grade.

Your BTEC First will cover either three or six units, depending on whether you are doing a Certificate or a Diploma. In this guide the activities cover Unit 1 'The Body in Sport' and Unit 3 'The Sports Industry'. These units underpin your study of sport.

Because the guide covers only two units, it is important that you do all the other work your tutor sets you. Your tutor will ask you to research information in textbooks, in the library and on the internet. You may also have your own textbook for the course: use it! You should have the chance to visit local organisations or welcome guest speakers to your institution. This is a great way to find out more about your chosen vocational area – the type of jobs that are available and what the work is really like.

This guide is a taster, an introduction to your BTEC First. Use it as such, and make the most of the rich learning environment that your tutors will provide for you. Your BTEC First will give you an excellent base for further study, a broad understanding of sport and the knowledge you need to succeed in the world of work.

Your BTEC First

Starting a new course is often both exciting and scary. It's normally exciting to do something new, and this includes learning different subjects that appeal to you. BTEC First courses are work-related, so you will be focusing on the work area that interests you. It can be nerve-wracking, though, if you are worried that there may be some topics that you will not understand, if you are unsure how you will be assessed, or if the prospect of some aspects of the course – such as finding out information on your own, or giving a presentation – makes your blood run cold!

It may help to know that these are worries common to many new BTEC First students. Yet every year thousands of them thoroughly enjoy their courses and successfully achieve the award.

Some do this the easy way, while others find it harder.

The easy way involves two things:

- knowing about the course and what you have to do

- positive thinking

Knowledge of the course means that you focus your time and energy on the things that matter. Positive thinking means that you aren't defeated before you start. Your ability to do well is affected by what goes on in your mind. A positive attitude helps you to meet new challenges more easily.

This guide has been written to give you all the information you need to get the most out of your course, to help you to develop positive thinking skills, and, of course, to help you successfully achieve your award. Keep it nearby throughout your course and re-read the relevant parts whenever you need to.

DO THINK	DON'T THINK
I'm quite capable of doing well on this course. First I need to check what I know about it and what I don't – and to fill in the gaps.	*If I struggle a bit or don't like something then so what? I can always drop out if I can't cope.*

Knowing about your course

If a friend or relative asked about your course, what would you say? Would you just shrug or give a vague comment? Or could you give a short, accurate description? If you can do this it usually means that you have a better understanding of what your course is all about – which means you are likely to be better prepared and better organised. You are also more likely to make links between your course and the world around you. This means you can be alert to information that relates to the subject you are studying.

→   Your family, friends, or other people you know may talk about topics that you are covering in class.

→   There may be programmes on television which relate to your studies.

→   Items in the news may be relevant.

→   You may work in a part-time job. Even if your part-time work is in a different area, there will still be useful links. For example, for most BTEC First courses you need to know how to relate to other people at work, how to assist your customers or clients and how to communicate properly. These are skills you need in most part-time jobs.

If you have only a hazy idea about your course then it is sensible to re-read any information you have been given by your school or college and to check further details on the Edexcel website at www.edexcel.org.uk. At the very least, you should know:

• the type of BTEC award you are aiming for and how many units you will be taking:

◊   BTEC First Diploma – normally taken as a full-time course, with six units

◊   BTEC First Certificate – may be taken as a full-time or part-time course, with three units

• the titles of your core units and what they cover

• the number of specialist units you must take and the options available to you

Core units are compulsory for all students at all centres, and you can find details of them on the Edexcel website. The range of specialist units you can choose will depend upon which award you are taking and where you are studying. Many centres design their courses to meet the needs of the students in their area, in which case you won't have complete freedom to choose your own options. If you do have a choice, find out the content of each of the specialist units available, then think carefully about the ones you would most like to study. Then talk through your ideas with your tutor before you make a final decision.

DO THINK	DON'T THINK
The more I know about my course, the more I can link the different parts together and see how they relate to other areas of my life. This will give me a better understanding of the subjects I am studying.	*It's unlikely that any course will have much relevance to my life or my interests, no matter what anyone says.*

Knowing the difference: BTEC First versus GCSE

BTEC First awards are different from GCSEs in several ways. In addition to the differences in content, the way the topics are taught and the tutors' expectations of their students are also often different. Knowing about these gives you a better idea of what to expect – and how you should respond.

→ BTEC First awards are work-related. All the topics you learn relate to the skills and knowledge you will need in the workplace.

→ They are practical. You will learn how to apply your knowledge, both on your own and as a member of a team, to develop your skills and abilities.

→ Most full-time BTEC First Diploma courses in colleges are completed in one year. If you are taking a BTEC First Certificate course alongside your GCSEs, then you will probably be doing this over two years.

→ There are no exams. So you won't be expected to revise and learn lots of facts, or to write answers to questions in a hot exam room next June. Instead, you will complete assignments set by your tutors, based on learning outcomes set by Edexcel. You can read more about assignments on page 19, but for now you can think of them as being similar to coursework. They will be given to you through the year, and each will have a deadline. See page 19 for advice on coping with assignments, and page 9 for advice on managing your time effectively.

→ On a BTEC First course you will achieve Pass, Merit and Distinctions in your assignments. You will then be awarded an overall Pass, Merit or Distinction for the whole course.

→   BTEC First students are encouraged to take responsibility for their own learning. Your tutors won't expect to have to stand over you all the time to check what you are doing. This helps you to develop the skills to be mature and independent at work. You will be expected to be keen and interested enough to work hard without being continually monitored. You will also be expected to become more self-reliant and better organised as the course progresses. Some students thrive in this situation. They love having more freedom, and are keen to show that they can handle it, especially when they know that they can still ask for help or support when they need it. Other students – thankfully, a minority – aren't mature enough to cope in this situation, so it goes to their head and they run wild.

→   If you've just left school and are going to study for your BTEC First in a college, then you will find many other differences. No bells or uniforms! Maybe fewer timetabled hours; probably longer lesson periods. You will mix with a wider range of people, of different ages and nationalities. You are starting a whole new phase of your life, when you will meet new people and have new experiences. However strange it may seem at the beginning, new students normally settle down quickly. Even if they have been disappointed with some of their grades at GCSE, they are relieved that they can put this disappointment behind them and have a fresh start. If this applies to you, then it's up to you to make the most of it.

DO THINK

On my BTEC First course I can find out more about the area of work that interests me. I will enjoy proving that I can work just as well with less direct supervision, and know I can get help and support when I need it.

DON'T THINK

Doing a BTEC First will be great because the tutors won't be breathing down my neck all the time and won't care if I mess around on the course.

Knowing how to use your time

How well organised are you? Do you always plan in advance, find what you've put away, and remember what you've promised to do without being reminded? Or do you live for the moment – and never know what you will be doing more than six hours in advance? Would you forget who you were, some days, unless someone reminded you?

School teachers cope with young students like this by giving homework on set nights, setting close deadlines, and regularly reminding everyone when work is due. They don't (or daren't!) ask students to do something over the next couple of months and then just leave them to it.

Although your BTEC First tutor will give you reminders, he or she will also be preparing you for higher-level courses and for having a responsible job – when you will be expected to cope with a range of tasks and deadlines with few, if any, reminders. On your BTEC First course some work will need to be completed quickly and done for the next session. But other tasks may take some time to do – such as finding out information on a topic, or preparing a presentation. You may be set tasks like this several weeks in advance of the deadline, and it can be easy to put them off, or to forget them altogether – with the result that you may not do the task at all, or end up doing a sloppy job at the last minute because you haven't had time to do it properly.

This problem gets worse over time. At the start of a new course there always seems to be a lot of time and not much pressure: the major deadlines may seem far in the future, and you may find it easy to cope day by day.

This situation is unlikely to last. Some tasks may take you longer than you had thought. Several tutors may want work completed at the same time. And deadlines have a nasty habit of speeding up as they approach. If you have lots of personal commitments too, then you may struggle to cope, and get very stressed or be tempted to give up.

The best way to cope is to learn to manage your own time, rather than letting it manage you. The following tips may help.

→ Expect to have work to do at home, both during the week and at weekends, and plan time for this around your other commitments. It's unrealistic to think that you can complete the course without doing much at home.

→ Schedule fixed working times into your week, taking your other commitments into account. For example, if you always play five-a-side football on Monday evening, keep Tuesday evening free for catching up with work. Similarly, if you work every Saturday, keep some time free on Sunday for work you have to complete over the weekend.

→ Get into the habit of working at certain times, and tell other people in your life what you are doing. If you've no work to do on one of these days, then that's a bonus. It's always easier to find something to do when you unexpectedly have free time than to find time for a task you didn't expect.

→ Write down exactly what you have to do in a diary or notebook the moment you are told about it, so that you don't waste time doing the wrong thing – or ringing lots of people to find out if they know what it is you're supposed to be doing.

→ Normally you should do tasks in order of urgency – even if this means you can't start with the one you like the best. But if, for example, you need to send off for information and wait for it to arrive, you can use the time to work on less urgent tasks.

→ Don't forget to include in your schedule tasks that have to be done over a period of time. It's easy to forget these if you have lots of shorter deadlines to meet. Decide how long the whole task is likely to take you, break the total time up into manageable chunks, and allocate enough time to complete it by the deadline date.

→ Always allow more time than you think you will need, never less.

→ Be disciplined! Anyone who wants to get on in life has to learn that there are times when you have to work, even if you don't want to. Try rewarding yourself with a treat afterwards.

→ If you are struggling to motivate yourself, set yourself a shorter time limit and really focus on what you are doing to get the most out of the session. You may be so engrossed when the time is up that you want to carry on.

→ Speak to your tutor promptly if you have a clash of commitments or a personal problem that is causing you serious difficulties – or if you have truly forgotten an important deadline (then vow not to do so again)!

→ If few of these comments apply to you because you are well organised, hard-working and regularly burn the midnight oil trying to get everything right, then don't forget to build leisure time and relaxation into your schedule. And talk to your tutor if you find that you are getting stressed out because you are trying too hard to be perfect.

<table>
<tr><td align="center">**DO THINK**</td><td align="center">**DON'T THINK**</td></tr>
<tr><td align="center">*I am quite capable of planning and scheduling the work I have to do, and being self-disciplined about doing it. I don't need a tutor to do this for me.*</td><td align="center">*I can only work when I'm in the mood and it's up to my tutors to remind me what to do and when.*</td></tr>
</table>

Knowing about resources

Resources for your course include the handouts you are given by your tutor, the equipment and facilities at your school or college (such as the library and resource centre), and information you can obtain on the internet from websites that relate to your studies. Resources that are essential for your course – such as a computer and access to the internet – will always be provided. The same applies to specialist resources required for a particular subject. Other resources – such as paper, file folders and a pen – you will be expected to provide yourself.

→   Some popular (or expensive) resources may be shared, and may need to be reserved in advance. These may include popular textbooks in the library, and laptop computers for home use. If it's important to reserve this resource for a certain time, don't leave it till the last minute.

→   You can only benefit from a resource if you know how to use it properly. This applies, for example, to finding information in the library, or using PowerPoint to prepare a presentation. Always ask for help if you need it.

→   You cannot expect to work well if you are forever borrowing what you need. Check out the stationery and equipment you need to buy yourself, and do so before the course starts. Many stationers have discounts on stationery near the start of term.

→   Look after your resources, to avoid last-minute panics or crises. For example, file handouts promptly and in the right place, follow the guidelines for using your IT system, and replace items that are lost or have ceased to work.

DO THINK	DON'T THINK
I have all the resources I need for my course, and I know how to use them or how to find out.	*I can find out what's available if and when I need it, and I can always cadge stuff from someone else.*

Knowing how to get the most from work experience

On some BTEC First courses – such as Children's Care, Learning and Development – all students must undertake a related work placement. On others, work placements are recommended but not essential, or may be required only for some specialist units. So whether or not you spend time on work experience will depend upon several factors, including the course you are taking, the units you are studying, and the opportunities in your own area. You will need to check with your tutor to find out whether you will be going on a work placement as part of your course.

If you need evidence from a work placement for a particular unit, then your tutor will give you a log book or work diary, and will help you to prepare for the experience. You should also do your best to help yourself.

Your placement

→ Check you have all the information about the placement you need, such as the address, start time, and name of your placement supervisor.

→ Know the route from home and how long it will take you to get there.

→ Know what is suitable to wear, and what is not – and make sure all aspects of your appearance are appropriate to your job role.

→ Know any rules, regulations or guidelines that you must follow.

→ Check you know what to do if you have a problem during the placement, such as being too ill to go to work.

→ Talk to your tutor if you have any special personal worries or concerns.

→   Understand why you are going on the placement and how it relates to your course.

→   Know the units to which your evidence will apply.

→   Check the assessment criteria for the units and list the information and evidence you will need to obtain.

DO THINK	DON'T THINK
Work experience gives me the opportunity to find out more about possible future workplaces, and link my course to reality.	*Work experience just means I'll be given all the boring jobs to do.*

Knowing how to get the most from special events

BTEC First courses usually include several practical activities and special events. These make the work more interesting and varied, and give you the opportunity to find out information and develop your skills and knowledge in new situations. They may include visits to external venues, visits from specialist speakers, and team events.

Some students enjoy the chance to do something different, while others can't see the point. It will depend on whether or not you are prepared to take an active involvement in what is happening. You will normally obtain the most benefit if you make a few preparations beforehand.

→   Listen carefully when any visit outside school or college, or any arrangement for someone to visit you, is being described. Check you understand exactly why this has been organised and how it relates to your course.

→   Find out what you are expected to do, and any rules or guidelines you must follow, including any specific requirements related to your clothes or appearance.

→   Write down all the key details, such as the date, time, location, and names of those involved. Always allow ample time so that you arrive five minutes early for any special event, and are never late.

→   Your behaviour should be impeccable whenever you are on a visit or listening to a visiting speaker.

→ Check the information you will be expected to prepare or obtain. Often this will relate to a particular assignment, or help you understand a particular topic in more detail.

→ For an external visit, you may be expected to write an account of what you see or do, or to use what you learn to answer questions in an assignment. Remember to take a notebook and pen with you, so that you can make notes easily.

→ For an external speaker, you may be expected to prepare a list of questions as well as to make notes during the talk. Someone will also need to say 'thank you' afterwards on behalf of the group. If your class wants to tape the talk, it's polite to ask the speaker for permission first.

→ For a team event, you may be involved in planning and helping to allocate different team roles. You will be expected to participate positively in any discussions, to talk for some (but not all) of the time, and perhaps to volunteer for some jobs yourself.

→ Write up any notes you make during the event neatly as soon as possible afterwards – while you can still understand what you wrote!

DO THINK	**DON'T THINK**
I will get more out of external visits, visiting speakers and team events if I prepare in advance, and this will also help me to get good grades.	*Trips out and other events are just a good excuse to have a break and take it easy for bit.*

Knowing how to find out information

Many students who are asked to find out information find it difficult to do so effectively. If they are online, they often print out too much, or can't find what they want. Similarly, too many students drift aimlessly around a library rather than purposefully search for what they need.

Finding out information is a skill that you need to learn. You need to know where to look, how to recognise appropriate information, and when to stop looking in order to meet your deadline, as well as what to do with the information when you've found it.

The first thing to realise is that you will never be asked to find out information for no reason. Before you start, you need to know what you are looking for, why it is needed, where you can find it, and the deadline.

This means you target your search properly and start looking in the right place.

Researching in the library

→   Find out the order in which books are stored. This is normally explained to all students during their induction.

→   Know the other resources and facilities that are available in your library besides books – for example, CD-ROMs and journals.

→   Take enough change with you so that you can photocopy articles that you can't remove. Remember to write down the source of any article you photocopy.

→   If you need specific books or articles, and aren't sure where they will be, try to visit during a quiet time, when the librarian can give you help if you need it.

→   If you find two or three books which include the information you need, that's normally enough. Too many can be confusing.

→   Check quickly if a book contains the information you need by looking in the index for the key words and then checking you can understand the text. If you can't, then forget it and choose another. A book is only helpful to you if you can follow it.

Researching online

→   Use a good search engine to find relevant websites. Scroll down the first few pages of the search results and read the descriptions to see which sites seem to be the best.

→   Remember to read all parts of the screen to check what's available on a website, as menus may be at the foot of the page as well as at the top or on either side. Many large sites have a search facility or a site map which you can access if you are stuck.

→   Don't get distracted by irrelevant information. If your searches regularly lead nowhere, ask your IT resource staff for help.

→   Don't print out everything you read. Even if printouts are free, too much information is just confusing.

→   Bookmark sites you use regularly and find helpful.

Researching by asking other people

This doesn't mean asking someone else to do the work for you! It means finding out about a topic by asking an expert.

→ Think about the people you know who might be able to help you because they have knowledge or experience that would be useful.

→ Prepare in advance by thinking about the best questions to ask.

→ Then contact the person and (unless you know the person well) introduce yourself.

→ Explain politely and clearly why you need the information.

→ Ask your questions, but don't gabble or ask them too quickly.

→ Write notes, so that you don't forget what you are told. Put the name and title of the person, and the date, at the top of the first page.

→ Ask if you can contact the person again, in case there is anything you need to check. Write down their phone number or email address.

→ Remember to say 'thank you'.

Using your information

→ Keep all your information on a topic neatly in a labelled folder or file. If you think you might want to reuse the folder later, put the title on in pencil rather than ink.

→ Refresh your memory of the task by re-reading it before you start to sift the information. Then only select pages that are relevant to the question you have been asked. Put all the other paper away.

→ Remember that you will rarely just be asked to reproduce the information that you have obtained. You will need to make decisions about which parts are the most relevant and how you should use these. For example, if you have visited a sports facility to find out what is available, then you may have to explain which activities are targeted at certain groups of people. You would be expected to disregard information that didn't relate to that task. Or you may be asked to evaluate the facilities, in which case you would have to consider how well the centre met the needs of its users and how it could do better.

→ Never rewrite copied information and pretend they are your own words! This is plagiarism, which is a serious offence with severe penalties. You need to state the source of your material by including the name of the author or the web address – either in the text, or as part of a list at the end. Your tutor will show you how to do this if you are not sure.

→ Write a draft and then ask your tutor to confirm that you are on the right track. You can also check with your tutor if you are unsure whether or not to include certain types of information.

DO THINK	DON'T THINK
Researching can be fun, and practice makes perfect. If I'm struggling to find something or to know what to include, I'll ask for help. Then it will be easier next time.	*The more I find the better, because collecting or writing a lot always impresses people.*

Knowing how to make a presentation

Presentations are a common feature of many BTEC courses. Usually you will be asked to do a presentation as a member of a team. If the team works together and its members support each other then this is far less of an ordeal than it may first seem. The benefits are that you learn many skills, including how to be a team member, how to speak in public, and how to prepare visual aids (often using PowerPoint) – all of which are invaluable for your future career.

Many students get worried about the idea of standing up to speak in front of an audience. This is quite normal, and can even improve your performance if you know how to focus your anxieties productively!

Presentation tasks can be divided into three stages: the initial preparations, the organisation, and the delivery.

Preparation

→   Divide up the work of researching fairly among the team.

→   Bear in mind people's individual strengths and weaknesses and allow for these, so that you all gain from working as a team.

→   Work out how long each person must speak so that you don't exceed your time limit (either individually or as a team).

→   Agree on the type of visual aids that would be best, given your topic. Keeping things simple is often more effective than producing something elaborate that doesn't work properly.

→   Decide on any handouts that are required, prepare these and check them carefully.

→   Check you know when and where the presentation will be held and what you should wear.

→ Think in advance about any questions you may be asked, both individually and as a team.

Organisation

→ Decide who will start and how each person will be introduced. Sometimes the lead person introduces everyone; on other occasions people introduce themselves.

→ Decide the most logical order in which to speak, bearing in mind everyone's contribution and how it fits into the overall presentation.

→ Prepare prompt cards. It's easy to forget some of the things you want to say, so put your main points down in the right order on a prompt card. Never read from this! Instead, write clearly and neatly so that you can just glance down to check on your next point.

→ Check you have sufficient copies of any handouts, and that these are clear and easy to read.

→ Rehearse several times and check your timings.

→ Get your clothes ready the night before.

→ Arrive at the event in plenty of time so that you're not in a rush.

Delivery

→ Take a few deep breaths before you start, to calm your nerves.

→ Make eye contact with your audience, and smile.

→ Keep your head up.

→ Speak a little more slowly than usual.

→ Speak a little more loudly than usual – without shouting.

→ Answer any questions you are asked. If you don't know the answer, be honest – don't guess or waffle.

→ Offer to help a team member who is struggling to answer a question, if you know the answer.

<table>
<tr><td>DO THINK</td><td>DON'T THINK</td></tr>
<tr><td>If I am well prepared and organised then my presentation will be OK, even if I'm really scared. The audience will always make allowances for some nerves.</td><td>I'm confident about speaking in public so I don't have to bother preparing in advance.</td></tr>
</table>

Knowing the importance of assignments

All BTEC First students are assessed by means of assignments. Each assignment is designed to link to specific learning outcomes. Assignments let you demonstrate that you have the skills and knowledge to get a Pass, Merit or Distinction grade. At the end of your course, your assignment grades together determine the overall grade for your BTEC First Certificate or Diploma.

Each assignment you are given will comprise specific tasks. Many will involve you in obtaining information (see page 14) and then applying your new-found knowledge to produce a written piece of work. Alternatively, you may demonstrate your knowledge by giving a presentation or taking part in an activity.

To get a good grade, you must be able to produce a good response to assignments. To do so, you need to know the golden rules that apply to all assignments, then how to interpret your instructions to get the best grade you can.

The golden rules for assignments

→ Read your instructions carefully. Check that you understand everything, and ask your tutor for help if there is anything that puzzles or worries you.

→ Check that you know whether you have to do all the work on your own, or if you will have to do some as a member of a group. If you work as a team, you will always have to identify which parts are your own contribution.

→ Write down any verbal instructions you are given, including when your tutor is available to discuss your research or any drafts you have prepared.

→ Check you know the date of the final deadline and any penalties for not meeting this.

→ Make sure you know what to do if you have a serious personal problem and need an official extension. An example would be if you were ill and expected to be absent for some time.

→ Remember that copying someone else's work (plagiarism) is always a serious offence – and is easy for experienced tutors to spot. Your school or college will have strict rules which state the consequences of doing this. It is never worth the risk.

→ Schedule enough time for finding out the information and making your initial preparations – from planning a presentation to writing your first draft or preparing an activity.

→ Allow plenty of time between talking to your tutor about your plans, preparations and drafts and the final deadline.

Interpreting your instructions to get the best grade you can

→ Most assignments start with a command word – for example, 'describe', 'explain' or 'evaluate'. These words relate to the level of answer required. A higher level of response is required for a Merit grade than for a Pass, and a higher level still for a Distinction.

→ Students often fall short in an assignment because they do not realise the differences between these words and what they have to do in each case. The tables below show you what is usually required for each grade when you see a particular command word.

→ As you can see from the tables, to obtain a higher grade with a given command word (such as 'describe'), you usually need to give a more complex description or use your information in a different way. You can refer to the example answers to real assignments, and tutor comments, from page 57 onwards.

→ You can check the command words you are likely to see for each unit in the grading grid. It is sensible to read this carefully in advance, so that you know the evidence that you will have to present to obtain a Pass, Merit or Distinction grade.

→ Be prepared to amend, redraft or rethink your work following feedback from your tutor, so that you always produce work that you know is your best effort.

→ Learn how to record your achievement so that you can see your predicted overall grade. Your tutor will show you how to do this, using the Edexcel *Recording your Achievement* form for your subject.

The following tables show what is required to obtain a Pass, Merit and Distinction, for a range of different 'command words'. Generally speaking:

- To obtain a Pass grade, you must be able to show that you understand the key facts relating to a topic.

- To obtain a Merit grade, you must be able to show that, in addition to fulfilling the requirements for a Pass grade, you can also use your knowledge in a certain way.

- To obtain a Distinction grade, you must be able to show that, in addition to fulfilling the requirements for a Pass and a Merit grade, you can also apply your knowledge to a situation and give a reasoned opinion.

Obtaining a Pass

Complete...	Complete a form, diagram or drawing.
Demonstrate...	Show that you can do a particular activity.
Describe...	Give a clear, straightforward description which includes all the main points.
Identify...	Give all the basic facts which relate to a certain topic.
List...	Write a list of the main items (not sentences).
Name...	State the proper terms related to a drawing or diagram.
Outline...	Give all the main points, but without going into too much detail.
State...	Point out or list the main features.

Examples:

- *List the main features on your mobile phone.*

- *Describe the best way to greet a customer.*

- *Outline the procedures you follow to keep your computer system secure.*

Obtaining a Merit

Analyse...	Identify the factors that apply, and state how these are linked and how each of them relates to the topic.
Comment on...	Give your own opinions or views.
Compare... **Contrast...**	Identify the main factors relating to two or more items and point out the similarities and differences.
Competently use...	Take full account of information and feedback you have obtained to review or improve an activity.
Demonstrate...	Prove you can carry out a more complex activity.
Describe...	Give a full description including details of all the relevant features.
Explain...	Give logical reasons to support your views.
Justify...	Give reasons for the points you are making so that the reader knows what you are thinking.
Suggest...	Give your own ideas or thoughts.

Examples:

- *Explain why mobile phones are so popular.*

- *Describe the needs of four different types of customers.*

- *Suggest the type of procedures a business would need to introduce to keep its IT system secure.*

Obtaining a Distinction

Analyse...	Identify several relevant factors, show how they are linked, and explain the importance of each.
Compare... **Contrast...**	Identify the main factors in two or more situations, then explain the similarities and differences, and in some cases say which is best and why.
Demonstrate...	Prove that you can carry out a complex activity taking into account information you have obtained or received to adapt your original ideas.

Describe...	Give a comprehensive description which tells a story to the reader and shows that you can apply your knowledge and information correctly.
Evaluate...	Bring together all your information and make a judgement on the importance or success of something.
Explain...	Provide full details and reasons to support the arguments you are making.
Justify...	Give full reasons or evidence to support your opinion.
Recommend...	Weigh up all the evidence to come to a conclusion, with reasons, about what would be best.

Examples:

- *Evaluate the features and performance of your mobile phone.*

- *Analyse the role of customer service in contributing to an organisation's success.*

- *Justify the main features on the website of a large, successful organisation of your choice.*

<table>
<tr><th>DO THINK</th><th>DON'T THINK</th></tr>
<tr><td>Assignments give me the opportunity to demonstrate what I've learned. If I work steadily, take note of the feedback I get and ask for advice when I need it, there is no reason why I can't get a good grade.</td><td>If I mess up a few assignments it isn't the end of the world. All teachers like to criticise stuff, and I only wanted a Pass anyway.</td></tr>
</table>

Knowing what to do if you have a problem

If you are lucky, you will sail through your BTEC First with no major problems. Unfortunately, not every student is so lucky. Some may encounter personal difficulties or other issues that can seriously disrupt their work. If this happens to you, it's vitally important that you know what to do.

→ Check that you know who to talk to if you have a problem. Then check who you should see if that person happens to be away at the time.

→ Don't sit on a problem and worry about it. Talk to someone, in confidence, promptly.

→ Most schools and colleges have professional counselling staff you can see if you have a concern that you don't want to tell your tutor. They will never repeat anything you say to them without your permission.

→ If you have a serious complaint, it's a good idea to talk it over with one of your tutors before you do anything else. Schools and colleges have official procedures to cover important issues such as appeals about assignments and formal complaints, but it's usually sensible to try to resolve a problem informally first.

→ If your school or college has a serious complaint about you, it is likely to invoke its formal disciplinary procedures, and you should know what these are. If you have done something wrong or silly, remember that most people will have more respect for you if you are honest about it, admit where you went wrong and apologise promptly. Lying only makes matters worse.

→ Most students underestimate the ability of their tutors to help them in a crisis – and it's always easier to cope with a worry if you've shared it with someone.

DO THINK	DON'T THINK
My tutors are just as keen for me to do well as I am, and will do everything they can to help me if I have a problem.	*No one will believe I have a problem. Tutors just think it's an excuse to get out of working.*

Finally...

This introduction wasn't written just to give you another task to do! It was written to help you to do your best and get the most out of your course.

So don't just put it on one side and forget about it. Go back to it from time to time to remind yourself about how to approach your course. You may also find it helpful to show it to other people at home, so that they will understand more about your course and what you have to do.

Activities

1   The skeletal system

In this section we will focus on grading criteria P1, P2, M1 and M2 from Unit 1 'The Body in Sport'.

You will explore the structure and function of the skeletal system, and how it changes as a result of physical activity. You will learn about the major bones and joints in the body, and understand how they work in different sporting movements. Case studies will help you identify the effects of exercise on the body in real-life sporting situations.

Learning outcomes

Understand the skeleton and how it is affected by exercise

Content

Structure of the skeletal system: bones (skull, sternum, ribs, vertebral column, clavicle, scapula, humerus, radius, ulna, pelvis, femur, tibia, fibula, patella); joints, classifications (fixed, slightly moveable, freely moveable/synovial), synovial joints (types, structure, function and range of movement)

Function of the skeletal system: protection; movement; shape; support; blood production; bone growth e.g. osteoblasts, osteoclasts, epiphyseal plate, physiological zones of bone growth

Movement: flexion; extension; adduction; abduction; rotation; examples from relevant sporting movements e.g. the effects of speed on posture

Effects of exercise: long and short-term effects; on bones e.g. increase in bone density; on synovial joints e.g. increased thickness of hyaline cartilage, greater production of synovial fluid

Grading criteria

P1: describe the structure and function of the skeleton, and how bones grow

You will gain an understanding of the structure and function of the human skeleton by looking closely at bones and joints. This will involve identifying the 14 major bones and understanding the three classifications of joints, paying particular attention to synovial joints and the range of movements they can produce in sporting contexts.

In addition, you will consider how the skeleton provides protection, movement, shape, support and blood production and how bones grow.

P2: identify the effects of exercise on bones and joints

You need to understand joint movement in terms of flexion, extension, adduction, abduction and rotation, and be able to apply these to real-life sporting actions, considering how various factors (such as speed) may affect them. You will study the effects of exercise on bones and joints in both the short and long terms.

M1: identify the movement occurring at synovial joints during three different types of physical activity

You will examine the three different sporting movements in terms of joints, and investigate other relevant factors such as weight bearing.

M2: explain the effects of exercise on bones and joints

You will begin to formulate ideas on the advantages and disadvantages of exercise for the bones and joints, incorporating knowledge of hyaline cartilage density and the production of synovial fluid.

Activity 1

Task 1

The adult skeleton consists of 206 bones. That's a lot to remember, so we're going to focus on the 14 major bones that you need to be able to identify when analysing sporting movements. Firstly, we're going to split the skeleton into three sections:

- body
- arm
- leg

Look at the three diagrams and identify which section of the skeleton they represent. Then use the list of bones on the right to label the bones in each section.

You can use the internet or your library to improve your knowledge and check your answers.

Bone names

- femur
- humerus
- tibia
- fibula
- ulna
- skull
- clavicle
- patella
- radius
- scapula
- sternum
- ribs
- vertebral column
- pelvis

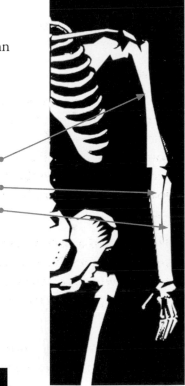

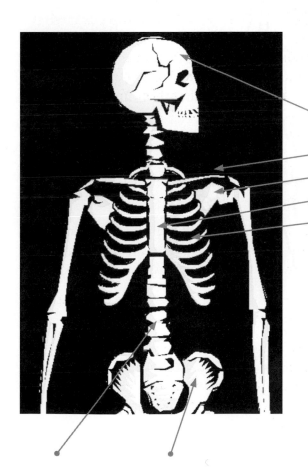

Task 2

Give yourself 30 seconds to look at your answers above. Remember them, and then give yourself a further 60 seconds to label the skeleton below, without looking at your previous answers.

Exchange your work with a partner and get them to check your results.

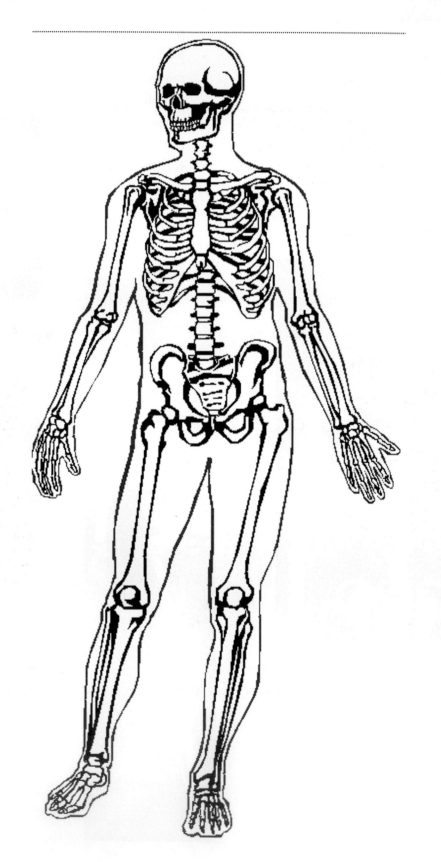

Activity 2

These bones don't just float around our bodies. They are attached to one another. A place where one bone meets another is called a joint, and strong bands called ligaments hold the joints and bones together. Some joints allow a great deal of movement; others allow none at all.

There are three basic types of joint:

- fixed joints
- slightly moveable joints
- freely moveable (synovial) joints

Work with a partner. Share the research resources you used in Activity 1 (e.g. books, internet sites), and see if you can find any further information from these sources that relates to joints. Use this information to assist you in this activity.

Task 1

Look at the pictures below. In each case, decide whether the joints are fixed, slightly moveable or freely moveable (synovial). Circle your answers.

With your partner, go over your answers and give reasons for them.

Suture joint

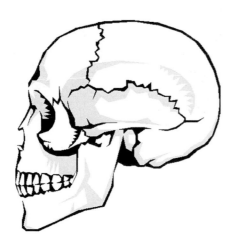

fixed
slightly moveable
freely movable (synovial)

Knee joint

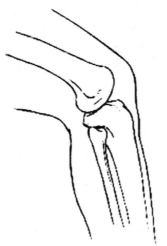

fixed
slightly moveable
freely movable (synovial)

Invertebral disc

fixed
slightly moveable
freely movable (synovial)

Task 2

Synovial joints allow the greatest range of movement: that's why we also refer to them as 'freely movable'. They are surrounded by synovial fluid. This is contained in a joint capsule and helps to protect and lubricate the moving parts of the joint. Synovial joints are used in nearly every sporting action.

Look at the six different synovial joints below. Copy the table into your workbook along with sketches of the joints. Use your research to complete the table. You will need to investigate each one in turn. Use sporting examples to help with your explanations.

Name	Description	Location in body	Range and type of movement (give a sporting example)
gliding joint			
hinge joint			
ball and socket joint			
condyloid			
pivot			
saddle			

Activity 3

The skeleton has many different functions that enable humans to live and survive. The main functions of the skeleton are protection, movement, shape, support, blood production and bone growth.

In groups, you are going to prepare a presentation for the rest of the class. It needs to be a simple and informative introduction to the main functions of the skeleton. Try to make it interesting and stimulating.

Presentations should provide everyone in the class with a variety of insights into the different functions of the skeleton. It is essential that when watching others' presentations you take part as an active listener and make notes on the areas you have not covered.

Each group should select one of the functions of the skeleton from the list below:

- protection
- movement
- shape
- support
- blood production

It is important that each member of the group is involved in preparing research for the presentation.

You could each work independently on a certain element before bringing your research together. Make sure that the workload is evenly split.

In your presentation, you should:

- identify at least three different bones, or group of bones, which you can use to help describe the function you are describing – for example, the skull and how it provides protection, or the femur and how it provides support
- try to provide sporting examples to help illustrate your descriptions

You have a total of 20 minutes for this task. You have 20 minutes to do your independent research and then 20 minutes to meet with the rest of your group, collate your ideas, and finalise your presentation. Each presentation should last between three and four minutes.

You can use visual aids (e.g. diagrams, pictures or video clips) to help with your presentation. You may find the following books useful:

- Stafford-Brown J et al., *BTEC First Sport: For Performance, Exercise and Fitness and Outdoor Recreation* (Hodder Arnold, 2006)
- Scott A, *GCSE PE for Edexcel* (Heinemann, 2001)

You may also find the GCSE Bitesize (Physical Education) website useful.

Activity 4

Another very important function of the skeleton is bone growth. The process of bone growth is called 'ossification', which continues until we are fully grown.

Growth only takes place in certain areas of our bones: these are called growth plates or 'epiphyseal plates'.

Task 1

Look at these X-ray photographs and see if you can identify the epiphyseal plates in each one. The first one shows the epiphyseal plates in the knee joint.

Task 2

Prepare a leaflet for children aged between 11 and 13, entitled 'Ossification', that informs them about bone growth. Choose one of the joints shown in the X-rays as your example.

Your target audience must be able to pick up your leaflet and understand how bones grow and where the growth takes place. Use colour and child-friendly language in your designs. You may wish to include graphics to help explain the following concepts:

- osteoblasts
- osteoclasts
- epiphyseal plates

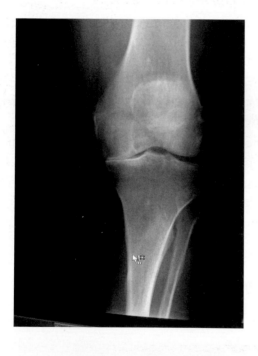

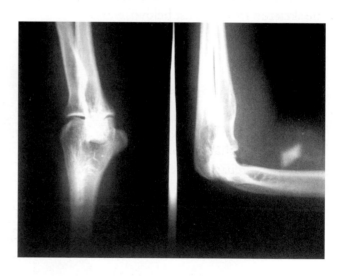

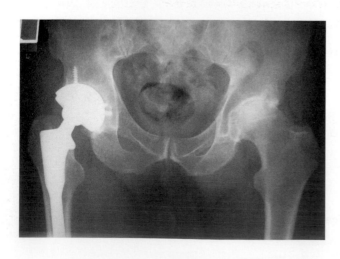

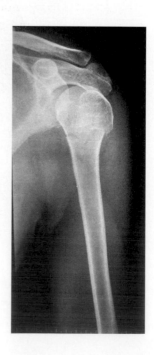

Activity 5

Sportspeople and their coaches need to have an understanding of how exercise affects our bodies.

Imagine you have been asked to compete for a lucrative contract to be the personal performance coach of one of the three sportspeople pictured on the following page. To win one of the contracts you will need to show that you know how to use your knowledge of the body in action. But competition for the contracts will be tough and you'll have to pitch for all three to have a fighting chance.

You will have to submit three separate performance reports to the agents. The reports need to focus on helping each performer understand how he or she can arrange training activities to have positive effects on bones and joints.

Be aware that these people participate in very different activities. You will need to appreciate their individual sports and the types of physical activity they involve. You will have to produce a personalised written report for each one. It will have to be handed to the agent by a specified deadline, and should be a clear summary of your findings and your recommendations.

Each report must include the following:

- Initial examination:
  - ◊ Identify the sport the person takes part in, describing key features of it.
  - ◊ Describe the types of movements used most often in their performances (e.g. kicking, throwing, running).
  - ◊ Consider the kinds of weight-bearing actions that occur in these movements.
  - ◊ Identify the synovial joints used in these movements, and explain the types of joint movement that they involve (e.g. flexion, extension, adduction, rotation).

- Research:
  - ◊ Identify the long- and short-term effects that weight-bearing actions may have on the performers' bones and joints. Pay close attention to those they use most often in their sport.
  - ◊ Explain these effects in terms of their advantages and disadvantages. What positive or negative effects could these have on the bones and joints?

- Recommendations:
  - ◊ Consider your initial assessment and research, and begin to draw some conclusions.
  - ◊ What activities would you recommend your sports performer to take part in during training sessions? Do these promote positive long- and short-term effects on the bones and joints? Explain your answers.
  - ◊ What activities would you recommend they avoid, if any? Give reasons.

You have an hour to complete this task. You should allow 20 minutes for each report. Your teacher will act as the representative sports agent to whom your reports will need to be handed. Don't be late, or you may lose out on that contract.

The internet may be a good source of information. Watching videos of your performer in action will help with your initial examination.

© Rai Sport

© Epoch Times

© Football Assn

2   The muscular system

In this section we will focus on grading criteria P3, P4, M3, D1 and D2 from Unit 1 'The Body in Sport'.

You will explore the structure and function of the muscular system, and how it changes as a result of physical activity. You will learn about the major muscles in the body, and understand how they work in different sporting movements. Case studies will help you identify the effects of exercise on the body in real-life sporting situations.

Learning outcomes

Understand the muscular system and how it is affected by exercise

Content

Major muscles: triceps; biceps; quadriceps; hamstrings; deltoids; gluteus maximus; gastrocnemius; abdominals; obliques; pectorals; trapezius; erector spinae; classification; location

Types of muscle: voluntary (skeletal); involuntary (smooth); heart (cardiac)

Muscle movement: tendons; antagonistic pairs; types of movement (concentric, eccentric, isometric)

Effects of exercise: short-term effects of exercise e.g. break down of muscle tissue; long-term effects of exercise e.g. hypertrophy

Grading criteria

P3: describe the different types of muscle, the major muscles in the body, and how muscles move

You will identify the major skeletal muscles and locate them on the human body, understanding how they differ from smooth (involuntary) and heart (cardiac) muscles. You will need to research all three types of muscle and analyse how they are controlled and moved.

P4: identify the effects of exercise on skeletal muscles

You will investigate the short- and long-term effects of exercise on the skeletal muscles.

M3: give examples of different types of muscular contraction relating to four different types of physical activity

Knowledge of movement will underpin the use of correct movement terms, identification of muscles, and visual demonstration of the direction of muscular forces across the appropriate joints.

D1: analyse four sporting movements, detailing the musculoskeletal actions occurring, and the contractions that are necessary

You will highlight the main actions, identifying antagonistic muscle pairs and the types of contraction taking place.

D2: analyse the effects of exercise on the musculoskeletal system

This will involve close examination of sporting movements, considering how training can influence movement by affecting the muscles and joints involved, and thinking about the short- and long-term effects of exercise and how they may improve or hinder sporting movement. You will incorporate advanced theories of anatomy and physiology in your analysis.

Activity 1

For this activity you will need three sheets of A4 paper (each one folded and then torn into quarter strips), and Blu-tack or sticky tape.

Task 1

With a partner, use the internet or books to locate a diagram of the human muscular system. Identify the following muscles:

- triceps
- biceps
- quadriceps
- hamstrings
- deltoids
- gluteus maximus
- gastrocnemius
- abdominals
- obliques
- pectorals
- trapezius
- erector spinae

As you identify each one of these twelve major muscles, write its name on a strip of paper in big clear letters.

You should end up with a stack of twelve muscle labels. Attach either sticky tape or Blu-tack to the back of each strip.

Task 2

Work in pairs. Put away your diagrams and hide any other notes you may have taken.

Have a go at attaching the muscle labels to the correct parts of your partner's body. You have one minute to do this.

Once your time is up, join up with another pair to make a group of four, and compare your results. Discuss them and make any necessary amendments.

Activity 2

You have three types of muscle in your body: smooth muscle, cardiac muscle and skeletal muscle. They all provide movement, but in different ways.

Imagine you are training to be team doctor for your favourite sports team. You will soon be asked to assist the coaching staff in their preparations for the upcoming world finals tournament. Your task will be to conduct the initial fitness assessments for all the players selected for the squad. During the assessments, you will need to identify and locate the three types of muscle in the body and check that they are all moving correctly.

But first, you must make sure you have a sound understanding of the different types of muscles and how they move. You will need to do some research and gain some practical experience.

Task 1

Find out:

- the differences between smooth, cardiac and skeletal muscle
- examples of all three types and where they are located in the body
- how each type of muscle moves, and how this movement is controlled

Copy out the table below to help you record your research.

Having completed this table, before you carry out the fitness assessments on the team, you should involve the players in the process and share your new-found knowledge.

Type of muscle	Description	Example	Location	How it moves	How it is controlled
smooth					
cardiac					
skeletal					

Task 2

Prepare a poster, to be displayed in the team's fitness centre, that describes the three different types of muscle and what they do. You may want to illustrate the poster with diagrams and pictures showing how the muscles move. Be sure to associate the movements with the team's sport, so that the players will relate to it more easily.

Useful words

- voluntary
- involuntary
- heart
- tendon
- antagonistic pair
- concentric movement
- eccentric movement
- isometric movement

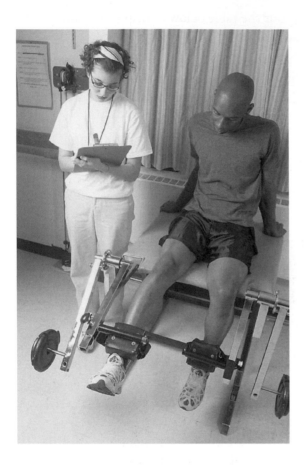

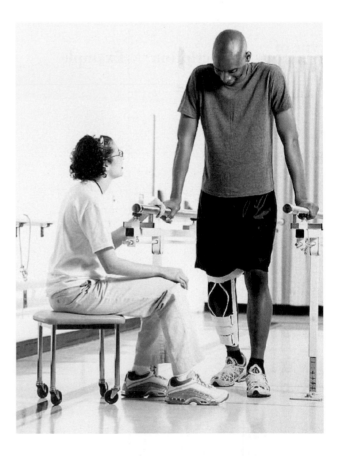

Activity 3

If you overload the muscles while training or exercising, particularly if you use some kind of resistance, such as weights, you will tear parts of the muscle tissue. This can be beneficial in building up your strength: if you combine your training with eating the correct foods, your body will begin to repair the damaged muscle tissue and gradually make it bigger and stronger than before.

This is the basic principle behind fitness training, especially when applied to body-building and strength training.

Imagine you are a personal trainer in a brand new city-centre health club. It has a state-of-the-art fitness centre with a great selection of free weights, machine weights and cardiovascular equipment. This has attracted a wide variety of people to take up membership to improve and maintain their fitness. Some of these people are associated with high-level amateur or semi-professional sports. You have already provided exercise and training programmes for a large proportion of these members.

A month has passed since opening, and some members have been working hard following the programmes you provided for them. Over the last few days, a couple of them have come to you with questions regarding their training, and require some feedback on how they are doing.

Task 1

Work in pairs. You will take turns to play the part of the personal trainer and the centre member seeking advice.

One of your members is a 21-year-old 100m sprinter who aspires to make the Great Britain team for the upcoming Olympics. His programme involved a great deal of heavy weight-lifting to gain strength and power in his arms and legs.

The sprinter requires answers to these questions:

- *What will have happened to my muscles in the first week of training?*
- *What state will my muscles be in now, a month into my programme?*
- *What will happen if I continue to train for another month?*

Set up a role-play where the sprinter arrives at the personal trainer's desk, and use the questions to spark a discussion between the two of you about the effects of the training programme on the sprinter.

Now swap roles, but continue the role-play. This time the sprinter wishes to ask some further questions:

- *Are there any challenges I may face in my training programme?*
- *Do I stay with the same programme all the time?*
- *What are the long-term advantages and disadvantages of my weight-training programme?*

Task 2

The sprinter is showing real promise. After a recent athletics meet, he has proved that he now has every chance of making the Olympic team. This has attracted the attention of the local media and a national athletics magazine. The magazine wishes to run a report about this up-and-coming star.

Take on the role of the magazine reporter. Use the information from your previous role-play discussions, and any additional information you may have, to write a report highlighting:

- the importance of exercise and training to improving the sprinter's fitness and performance
- the short- and long-term advantages and disadvantages of their training programme

Imagine you have already interviewed both the sprinter and the personal trainer at the gym. The interviews could be used as a basis for your report.

The report must be an individual piece of work of up to 400 words, and should be submitted to the editor (your teacher) by an agreed deadline.

Activity 4

Skeletal muscles allow sportspeople to move in many different, sometimes spectacular, ways. Muscles work in pairs. First one will contract, and then the other. This has the effect of pulling our bones back and forth, creating various types of muscular movement.

Muscle pairs are called 'antagonistic pairs'. They can produce concentric, eccentric and isometric movement and contraction.

Task 1

Divide into four or five groups.

Ideally, each group should have a video camera or digital still camera (with playback), and four willing volunteers.

Each group must select four different sporting movements from four different sports. It would be ideal to have available the correct equipment for each sport, but it's not essential. Ask your four volunteers to perform these four actions, and record them doing so several times. Watch them both live and on playback, and consider what muscles may be involved in these movements and what types of contractions may be occurring. If possible, use slow motion to see more detail. Make notes in your file.

Task 2

Imagine you are a member of the PE department at a secondary school. You have been asked to produce a wall display illustrating the different types of muscular contraction that can occur. So that it appeals to all pupils, the display must show a variety of different sporting movements from at least four sports. It should be simple and informative.

Put together a wall display that incorporates images, diagrams, and drawings as well as any necessary text. Other members of the department (your group) can help you, and you can work collaboratively on the project, but your display should be your own. Use what you have seen practically, and any video footage you may have. You can also use the library, the internet and the textbooks suggested below for your research.

Your display must include a clear description and illustration of four different movements, from four different sports, involving different contractions. For each movement you must explain:

- the type of contraction
- how the movement is brought about
- the antagonistic pairs
- the type of movement created about the joint

Agree a deadline with the head of department (your teacher).

Task 3

In recognition of the quality of your display, the head of department has asked you to present it to a group of GCSE students in a forthcoming revision class. Before you do this, you must first present it to the head of department, so that they are satisfied with it.

In addition to the wall display, you will have to prepare individually a five-minute presentation using PowerPoint, slides or a flipchart. This is therefore an opportunity to incorporate any additional visuals, such as images or video footage, you may have gathered in your research. You will then deliver your presentation to the head of department (your teacher).

Your presentation should describe:

- the musculoskeletal actions occurring in each movement
- the contractions necessary to bring about the movement
- how the two factors above bring about the desired movement
- how exercise and training may bring about any variations in the movement
- how the movement could be improved
- any risks of injury due to the movements and contractions

Suggested reading

- Stafford-Brown J et al., *BTEC First Sport: For Performance, Exercise and Fitness and Outdoor Recreation* (Hodder Arnold, 2006)
- Scott A, *GCSE PE for Edexcel* (Heinemann, 2001)
- Marieb E N, *Human Anatomy and Physiology*, 5th edition (Addison Wesley, 2001)

3   The nature of the sports industry

In this section we will focus on grading criteria P1, P2, M1 and D1 from Unit 3 'The Sports Industry'.

Learning outcome

Understand the nature of the sports industry

Content

Activities: e.g. team and individual games, gymnastic, dance, athletics, outdoor and adventurous activities

Provision: public sector e.g. local authority facilities; private sector e.g. private health clubs; voluntary sector e.g. voluntary sports clubs

Organisation: structure and function; governing bodies (national and international) e.g. International Olympic Committee, the Lawn Tennis Association, the Rugby Football Union

Development: trends e.g. participation, consumption

Growth: e.g. increased leisure time, fashion, increased disposable income

Grading criteria

P1: describe the local provision of sport

P2: describe the national provision of sport

This means that you will need to know exactly how and where sport is provided in your area, and where sport is played nationally by professionals and other elite athletes. You will need to research the facilities that offer sporting activities.

M1: compare local and national provision of sport, identifying areas for improvement

You will need to choose two sports facilities (one local and one national), look at which sector they belong to, and compare them – for example, their opening times, the number and age of the people using them, their usage trends through the year, the cost of activities, and the locations. You will also need to assess whether there are things they could be doing better.

D1: evaluate local and national provision of sport, suggesting ways in which local provision could be improved

You will need to look in detail at the strengths of the national provision for sport, and recommend what areas of provision could be adopted by local facilities. In examining a local facility you will need to point out any weaknesses and explain what it could do to improve its service.

Activity 1

Task 1

Working on your own, highlight the nine sporting activities hidden in this wordsearch. Words can be horizontal, vertical or diagonal, and can go in any direction.

W	B	R	G	T	S	O	O	S	W	S	Z
T	Z	V	N	R	C	I	H	P	E	T	J
P	X	V	I	A	V	A	N	C	I	R	R
D	N	U	R	M	T	U	N	N	K	A	A
V	W	J	E	P	A	A	L	E	E	D	T
N	K	T	E	O	D	G	O	L	F	T	H
Y	E	V	T	L	R	B	K	P	K	W	L
B	O	G	N	I	M	M	I	W	S	V	E
Y	F	R	E	N	A	M	J	H	I	A	T
W	D	R	I	I	J	W	D	U	E	S	I
N	M	J	R	N	N	D	Y	M	D	H	C
Y	I	Y	O	G	D	P	W	F	B	O	S

Task 2

Complete the next wordsearch with the help of a friend. There are seven words to find.

N	E	T	B	A	L	L	Q	R	B	E	Z
L	J	C	W	I	Q	U	U	A	M	S	L
M	L	X	J	L	X	G	S	O	W	S	Q
I	N	A	P	L	B	K	Y	G	G	O	H
L	L	A	B	Y	E	L	L	O	V	R	O
Y	Q	H	F	T	G	A	T	G	Z	C	C
O	A	W	B	P	O	E	G	U	M	A	K
L	L	A	Y	F	K	O	P	U	W	L	E
Z	L	J	Q	C	M	F	F	U	E	P	Y
L	L	E	I	N	T	N	O	I	N	U	E
U	R	R	J	C	Q	K	S	A	N	C	Z
I	C	G	Z	D	T	X	W	G	B	I	M

Task 3

Within your local area, facilities for these sports are provided by the public, private and voluntary sectors:

- Public sector
  - ◊ The public sector is funded partly by council tax and partly by grants from central government. Your local authority or council will run public-sector facilities as a service to people in your area. For example, they may provide sports and leisure centres, but this is not the only type of provision. Bracknell District Council is one of many that run a golf course. Hull City Council provides several skate parks, which are proving popular with the younger generation.
- Private sector
  - ◊ Private-sector organisations aim to make a profit. For example, they may provide health and fitness clubs.
- Voluntary sector
  - ◊ The voluntary sector is run by people who have a common interest and who give their time and energy for free. This allows them to join like-minded people and to be active in their chosen sport.

To find out more about these areas, you may find the following websites useful:

- www.ccpr.org.uk
- www.sportengland.org
- www.prospects.ac.uk

Using your results from the wordsearches, complete the table below. Research your area using the internet and Yellow Pages, and state whether facilities for each activity are provided by the public, private or voluntary sector (or a combination of these).

Discuss your answers as a class. Be prepared to justify them.

Activity	Sector		
	Public	Private	Voluntary

Activity 2

Divide into groups of six; then divide each group into three pairs. Each pair will be allocated a sector, and then organise a visit to a facility provided by that sector. You will need to contact the facility to arrange a time to visit.

- First pair: choose a facility run by your local authority. For example, this could be a swimming pool, leisure centre, tennis courts, or a park with a variety of sport facilities.
- Second pair: choose a facility from the private sector. For example, this could be a health club, a private tennis, squash or golf club, or any other sports club which people have to pay a fee to join.
- Third pair: choose a facility from the voluntary sector. For example, this could be a youth club, or a local football, rugby or netball team that is run on a voluntary basis.

You are going to be to find out about the facility, and decide what improvements, if any, could be made to it. Before you go on your visit, you will need to make a list of questions to be answered.

Task 1

As a class, brainstorm ideas for questions you might ask on a visit. You might want to find out about the clients, about busy times and slack times, and how clients get to the facility (whether there are there good public transport links and car parking facilities). Add anything you would like to know to the brainstorm.

Task 2

With your partner, devise a checklist. This will help you to record your answers in a simple format when you interview a member of staff at the leisure facility. An example is given below, but you may want to add other questions that arose from your brainstorm.

	Question	Information	Comments
1	Where is the facility located?		
2	Which sector or sectors does the facility belong to? Who owns it?		
3	What are the opening hours?		
4	Is there a membership fee?		
5	Are different types of membership available?		
6	How many people use the facility per day? Per month? Per year?		
7	How many members of staff are there at the facility?		
8	What are the job titles of the staff?		
9	Does the facility have a car park?		
10	Does the facility advertise? If so, where?		
11	What improvements would you like to see at the facility?		

Task 3

Organise your visit to the facility, and carry out your research. After your visit, remember to write a thank-you letter to the staff who helped you.

Task 4

In your group of six, make a short PowerPoint presentation to the rest of the class, describing the three facilities you visited and the activities that happen at them. You should describe any areas that need to be improved, why they need to be improved, and how. These might include access (road and public transport links), parking, pricing packages, publicity and marketing, and how the facility is used.

Activity 3

It is estimated that the new Wembley Stadium will attract over one and a half million spectators to football and rugby events each year. It will also be the country's leading venue for music concerts, and will enable the UK to attract world-class sporting events such as the Olympic Games, the football World Cup, and the World Athletics Championships.

Task 1

Go to www.wembleystadium.com and find out all you can about the new stadium. Find out about the building programme, the design of the stadium, and the facilities on offer. Make notes to bring to class. Other websites that might help your research include:

- www.bbc.co.uk
- www.sportsvenue-technology.com
- www.thefa.com

Task 2

As a whole class, carry out a SWOT analysis on the new Wembley Stadium. This means looking at the strengths, weaknesses, opportunities and threats:

Strengths	Weaknesses
What are the strengths of the facility? For example, state-of-the-art equipment, capacity, transport.	What are the weaknesses of the facility? For example, lack of funding.
Opportunities	**Threats**
What opportunities are there to improve or develop the facility?	Are there other facilities offering a similar range of activities that are in direct competition?

Task 3

On your own, decide how you would deal with the threats, and overcome any weaknesses of the new Wembley stadium. Produce a display to explain your ideas.

Task 4

Look back at the work you did for Activity 2, especially Task 4.

Bearing in mind what you have found out about the new Wembley Stadium, write a short letter to your local council suggesting how it could improve provision for sport in your area.

4   Participation in sport

In this section we will focus on grading criteria P6, M3 and D3 from Unit 3 'The Sports Industry'.

The activities will enable you to understand the various issues surrounding mass sports participation on a local and national scale. You will describe, explain and evaluate various strategies designed to improve sports participation. When you have completed the activities you will be able to decide if the strategies already in place are working, and if they can be improved.

Both the government and various sporting governing bodies have long-term action plans (or strategies) to get more people, young and old, taking part in sport. This is because sports participation is good for our physical and mental health. There are many initiatives, and an increase in the numbers of sports development officers within counties and local authorities. You will find out about the strengths and weaknesses of these initiatives, and you may discover where there is room for improvement.

Learning outcome

Understand how and why people participate in sport

Content

Ways: e.g. performer (amateur, professional), official, coach, leader, administrator, spectator, consumer, retailer, medical staff, sports development

Reasons: health and fitness benefits; social benefits; development (personal, skill)

Factors that affect participation: disability; provision; cost; ethnicity; location; age

Strategies to encourage participation: strategies e.g. mass participation (school sports strategies, government initiatives), sports specific schemes, sports development officers; strengths and weaknesses of strategies

Grading criteria

P6: describe ways in which participation in sport is encouraged

This means that you must have a clear understanding of the ways in which sport is encouraged, and be able to give a clear description of all the relevant features.

M3: explain strategies used by a chosen sport to encourage participation

You must identify strategies used for promoting a specific sport. You will need to understand the reasons behind the strategies, and be able to describe how they work and the reasons behind their introduction.

D3: evaluate strategies used by a chosen sport to encourage participation.

You need to look in detail at the sport you have chosen, and the initiatives that are in place to encourage more people to take part. You will need to form your own conclusions about how successful the strategies have been in meeting their aims, and back them up with solid evidence.

Activity 1

The London Marathon is a serious event, with large prize money attracting elite athletes. However, public perception of the race is dominated by the fun runners. Often in fancy dress and collecting money for charity, these make up a small but significant proportion of the 30,000 runners in the main event, and help to draw crowds of approximately half a million on the streets.

In 1979, hours after having run the New York Marathon, the former Olympic champion Chris Brasher wrote an article for the Observer which began: 'To believe this story you must believe that the human race be one joyous family, working together, laughing together, achieving the impossible. Last Sunday, in one of the most trouble-stricken cities in the world, 11,532 men and women from 40 countries in the world, assisted by over a million black, white and yellow people, laughed, cheered and suffered during the greatest folk festival the world has seen.' Enchanted with the sight of people coming together for such an occasion, he concluded questioning 'whether London could stage such a festival?'

Within months the London Marathon was born, with Brasher making trips to America to study the race organisation and finance of big city marathons such as New York and Boston, the oldest in the world. He secured a contract with Gillette of £50,000, established the organisation's charitable status, and set down six main aims for the event, which he not only hoped would echo the scenes he had witnessed in New York, but also put Britain firmly on the map as a country capable of organising major events.

His vision was realised on March 29th 1981, with the inaugural London Marathon proving an instant success. More than 20,000 people applied to run: 7,747 were accepted and 6,255 crossed the finish line on Constitution Hill as cheering crowds lined the route. Since this time the event has continued to grow in size, stature and popularity with a capacity 46,500 accepted entrants each year. In all, a total of 572,174 have completed the race since its inception with a record 32,899 crossing the line in 2002.

http://www.london-marathon.co.uk/site/ marathon_history/index.php?page=1

Task 1

Research the London Marathon using the internet. Produce a poster that explains why it is such a successful event. Look at what attracts people to participate, and how the organisers ensure that everyone enjoys the day.

Task 2

In pairs, think of a viable sporting event that you could host in your area. Think about how the event will be organised, and how you will encourage mass participation. With your partner, write a short press release for your local paper describing the event, then produce a poster or flyer promoting the event to likely participants.

© Gilbrit, Flickr

Activity 2

Task 1

Many sports benefit from mass participation. With increased publicity comes increased awareness and participation. This increases individual and national performance levels, giving a feel-good factor to all participants, as well as promoting good health.

Brainstorming in groups of four, think of as many sports as you can that benefit from mass participation.

Task 2

Choose two sports from your list. Your task is to find out what strategies are currently in place to increase participation in these sports.

To help you, here are four examples of current sporting initiatives. Each of these has its own specific strategy, each with slightly different aims. As a starting point, find out if these initiatives help your chosen sports.

- PE, School Sport and Club Links Initiative
- Get Into Football Campaign
- Sports Development Initiative
- Talented Athlete Scholarship Scheme 2012

Task 3

As a group, give a short presentation to your class about the four strategies listed above (or any others you've found out about). Your presentation must include a clear description of all of their main features.

Make notes from the presentations given by the rest of the class.

© Ulybug Photos, Flickr

Task 4

Working on your own, copy out and complete the table below.

To help you with your researches, you might visit the following websites:

- Schools Sports Strategy: www.culture.gov. uk/sport/school_sport
- Football: www.thefa.com/GrassrootsNew
- Talented Athlete Scholarship Scheme: www. culture.gov.uk/sport/tass_2012scholarships

For information on the Sports Development Initiative, contact your local sports development department. This may be within your council's education department, or leisure department, or another department, so you will have to do some research. In your description, focus on what is happening in your area.

Initiative	Brief description	Four major aims or benefits
PE, School Sport and Club Links Initiative		
Get Into Football Campaign		
Sports Development Initiative		
Talented Athlete Scholarship Scheme 2012		

Now describe the major strengths and weaknesses of the four schemes, explaining clearly why they are strengths or weaknesses.

Activity 3

Read the two case studies below. One is about football and the other tennis. If you are not interested in football or tennis, you may research a sport of your own choice.

Case study 1

Football is the national sport. There are many opportunities for people to be involved in the game. The following facts (taken from www.thefa. com) illustrate this.

There are 7 million participants, of whom 5 million play in schools.

Football is played in over 37,000 schools, of which 17,000 are primary schools.

In the UK there are over 30,000 FA-qualified coaches and 2,700 qualified referees.

The 2005 FA cup final was broadcast live to over 150 countries worldwide.

In 2005 there were over 45,000 football pitches at 21,000 different locations.

The Football Association, or FA (founded in 1863) is responsible for the organisation of the game in England. One of its major roles is to promote the game at both local and national levels. This is done by ensuring that there are opportunities for everyone to play, whatever their age, sex, ability, race, culture or background. The FA runs a number of campaigns aimed at promoting the sport and increasing levels of participation. One of the most easily recognisable is 'Get Involved'. Football is now the top female sport, and in the 2005–6 season 133,000 players competed in affiliated league and cup competitions. FA research has shown that over 1.5 million girls under the age of 15 played some form of football over the last 12 months. The FA funds 43 full-time officers specifically to develop opportunities for girls to play football.

© Colchester United Community Sports Trust

Case study 2

Tim Henman and former Wimbledon winner Boris Becker have lent their support to a scheme to find new British tennis talent.

They are involved in a programme run by the Lawn Tennis Association and washing powder maker Ariel aimed at introducing children of all backgrounds to tennis.

'We've seen over 10,000 kids. With the help of the LTA, we're now down to 20,' Becker told BBC Radio Five Live.

'The overall winners will get a chance to play tennis with myself and Tim.'

The two winners, a boy and a girl, will also get a year's free LTA tennis coaching and tennis equipment.

http://news.bbc.co.uk
© bbc.co.uk

Tennis has become an increasingly popular sport in the UK over the last 20 years. This is mainly thanks to Britain having two players ranked in the world's top 20 and the popularity of the Wimbledon tennis championships that take place each year. The governing body of tennis is the Lawn Tennis Association. Its job is to look out for up-and-coming talent, provide the necessary facilities, improve participation levels, promote the game, and generally look after the wellbeing and the best interests of tennis. The LTA works at county level so that tournaments can be arranged more easily and clubs can get individual attention appropriate to the needs of their geographical area.

As with all sports, the route to tennis stardom starts at grassroots level – which includes all recreational play. In particular, children need to be given the opportunity to play and maintain their interest in the game.

In order to increase participation levels, a number of strategies have been implemented. One such is the Ariel Tennis Challenge. The challenge is to find the next British tennis superstar.

Resources

- www.lta.org.uk
- www.arieltennis.com

© Tennisserver

Task

Choose one sporting campaign and answer the following questions:

- What are the aims of the campaign?
- How successful has the campaign been? Give your reasons.
- Does the campaign include all sections of the community? If so, how does it do this?
- Are there any possible areas for improvement? Say what these are and give examples of how they could be improved. What would be the effect of your suggested improvements?

Activity 4

Work either on your own or with a partner.

The marketing manager of a local sports centre, Kris Beddows, wants to encourage sports participation and has decided to organise fun weeks during the summer holidays for 11–18 year olds. Kris will be producing a leaflet to promote these weeks. He is undecided about what sports to run during the fun weeks, and would like to know more about the sporting strategies already in place.

Task 1

Decide on a sport that you think would be suitable for 11–18 year olds, and write an email to Kris explaining what strategies are in place for this sport.

Task 2

Draft an A4 leaflet that Kris can use to promote the fun weeks.

Activity 5

In groups of three, choose a sport that has strategies in place to increase participation.

Prepare a poster to show how successful the strategies have been for your chosen sport. You will have to decide how you measure the success of the strategies: you might want to include participation figures (perhaps presented as a graph or chart), a short case study, newspaper articles, pictures, high-profile figures supporting the schemes, and quotes and information on specific initiatives. Trevor Brooking, the FA's Director of Football Development, has led many schemes through the Football for the Disabled Strategy such as 'Ability Counts'.

Activity 6

Look at the pictures on these two pages. Then answer the following questions:

- What impact do the pictures have on you? Are you surprised to see people with physical disabilities actively participating in sport?

- Do you think that these pictures would encourage people with disabilities to participate in a particular sport? Give your reasons.

- Why do you think that the Football Association has launched a special strategy to encourage people with disabilities to participate in football?

- From your research, do you think that particular groups have been identified and targeted and drawn into sport in the community? What evidence do you have?

- Do you think that these schemes are successful? How could success be measured? How do the schemes measure up?

- Can you identify any possible areas for improvement in these schemes? What improvements might be made? What effect would these have?

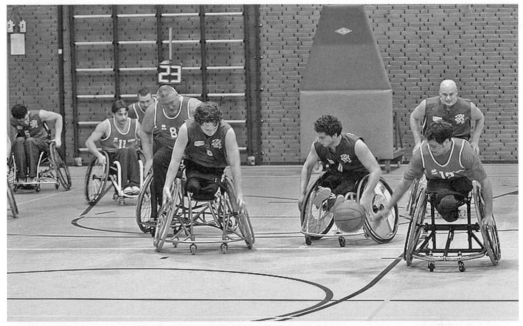

Answers to Activity 3.1 (p 43)

Task 1

W	B	R	G	T	S	O	O	S	W	S	Z
T	Z	V	N	R	C	I	H	P	E	T	J
P	X	V	I	A	V	A	N	C	I	R	R
D	N	U	R	M	T	U	N	N	K	A	A
V	W	J	E	P	A	A	L	E	E	D	T
N	K	T	E	O	D	G	O	L	F	T	H
Y	E	V	T	L	R	B	K	P	K	W	L
B	O	G	N	I	M	M	I	W	S	V	E
Y	F	R	E	N	A	M	J	H	I	A	T
W	D	R	I	I	J	W	D	U	E	S	I
N	M	J	R	N	N	D	Y	M	D	H	C
Y	I	Y	O	G	D	P	W	F	B	O	S

Task 2

N	E	T	B	A	L	L	Q	R	B	E	Z
L	J	C	W	I	Q	U	U	A	M	S	L
M	L	X	J	L	X	G	S	O	W	S	Q
I	N	A	P	L	B	K	Y	G	G	O	H
L	L	A	B	Y	E	L	L	O	V	R	O
Y	Q	H	F	T	G	A	T	G	Z	C	C
O	A	W	B	P	O	E	G	U	M	A	K
L	L	A	Y	F	K	O	P	U	W	L	E
Z	L	J	Q	C	M	F	F	U	E	P	Y
L	L	E	I	N	T	N	O	I	N	U	E
U	R	R	J	C	Q	K	S	A	N	C	Z
I	C	G	Z	D	T	X	W	G	B	I	M

Marked assignments

Exemplar assignment

Unit 1 – The Body in Sport

Produce an easy-to-follow article that will form part of a revision aid to assist the GCSE students at a local sports college with their anatomy and physiology revision for their up and coming examination.

Task 1 (P1, P2)

Describe (using diagrams when appropriate to support your descriptions) the structure and function of the skeleton. You must also include a description of how bones grow. (P1)

Identify the effects of exercise on bones and joints. (P2)

Task 2 (M2)

Explain the effects of exercise on bones and joints. (M2)

Task 3 (D2)

Analyse the effects of exercise on the musculoskeletal system. (D2)

Pass level answer

Margaret Harper – Task 1 (P1, P2)

The Skeleton

Margaret, a detailed diagram clearly identifying the skeletal system.

You need to label the scapula, but this is good evidence of external research.

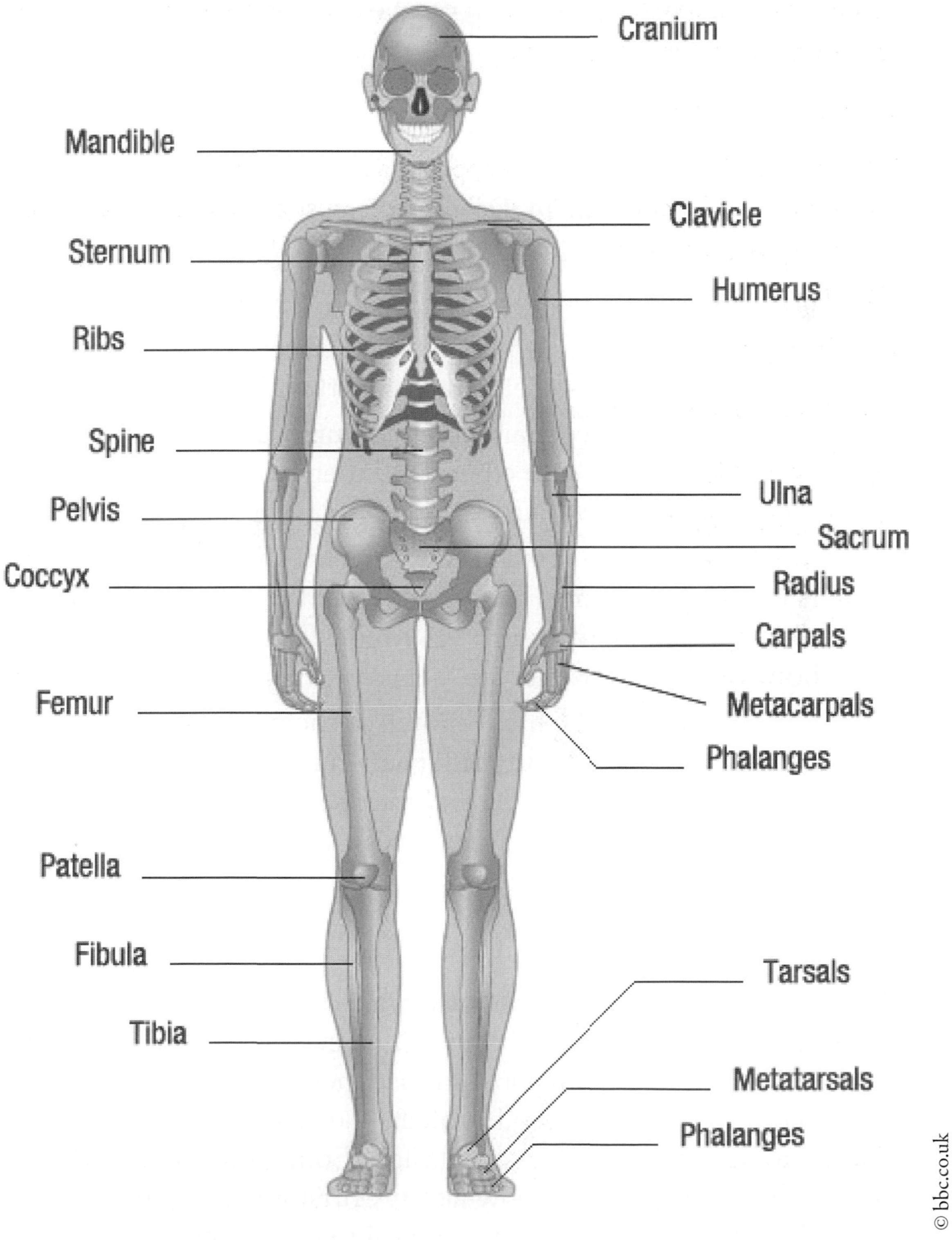

- Cranium
- Mandible
- Clavicle
- Sternum
- Humerus
- Ribs
- Spine
- Pelvis
- Ulna
- Sacrum
- Coccyx
- Radius
- Carpals
- Metacarpals
- Femur
- Phalanges
- Patella
- Fibula
- Tarsals
- Tibia
- Metatarsals
- Phalanges

© bbc.co.uk

Diagram 1: the human skeleton www.bbc.co/science

Our skeleton is made up of bones: our arms and legs, back and head. It is very important. Without it we would be floppy bags of skin. The bones are joined to each other at joints and we have muscles attached to our bones that allow us to move. We can move our arms up and down to eat, to throw balls, to hold hands. We can move our legs and so walk and run. We can do everything from tiny little movements with our head or fingers to giant strides with our legs and feet.

Bones of the skeleton

These are the main bones of the body:
- The skull which includes your face bones and jaw.
- The sternum which is down the middle of your chest.
- Ribs. We have 12 pairs of ribs and they are attached to the sternum at the front and our spine (or vertebral column) at the back. Your ribs protect your heart and lungs.
- Your arm has three main bones: a humerus which goes from your shoulder to your elbow and then two other bones, radius and ulna, which join onto your hand.
- The leg is like the arm and has three main bones. The femur is the big thigh bone, then at the knee there are two bones, tibia and fibula, that go to your foot. The knee joint has a bone over it, your kneecap, also called the patella.
- Other bones are the hips, known as the pelvis and the bones at the shoulder – the shoulder called the clavicle this is also known as the collar bone and the back of the shoulder is the scapula; this bone is also known as the should blade. These help attach the arm to the body.

> This description shows that you clearly know the major bones of the body but you do need to locate the scapula on your diagram of the skeleton.

The skeleton as protection

The skull protects the very delicate brain. But we shouldn't rely on just our skull to protect our brain. When cycling, for example, it's important to wear a helmet just in case there is an accident. The spinal column surrounds and protects the spinal cord (the nerves that go to our arms and legs and lungs). Sometimes that protection is not always perfect. We know about Christopher Reeves (Superman) who fell off a horse and injured his neck and spinal column, leaving him paralysed. Our ribs surround and protect our important organs like our lungs, stomach and liver. Our pelvis protects our lower intestine and sex organs and will protect unborn babies.

The skeleton for blood production

As well as giving us strength and support, our bones also carry out important functions. In the centre of our big bones there is marrow that produces white blood cells that we use to fight infections. We also make red blood cells in our bones. The red blood cells carry oxygen round our bodies.

The skeleton for storing minerals

Our bones also store minerals. The most important one is calcium because we use this to make our bones strong and grow them. If we don't have enough calcium, when we are old, our bones can break.

Our growing bones

Our bones grow until we are adults. When I was 11-years old I was 1.37 m tall. Now I am 1.65 m. My feet used to be 20.5 cm long and now they are 24 cm long. Our hands and feet begin to grow first, then our shin bones and lower arm bones, then our thighs and top arm bones grow. Finally shoulders and hips grow to give us our final shape.

Bones grow at their ends. At the end of long bones (like the femur) there is an area called the growth plate. This is cartilage and its cells (osteoblasts) divide like other cells and so grow. Eventually the cartilage cells die away and the space is filled in with bone. This is called ossification. In tiny babies, all their bones are soft and a bit like cartilage. As the cartilage gets older, the cells die and turn into bone. When a bone reaches its full size (at the end of puberty) all the growth plates turn into bone and you don't grow anymore.

This is a good description of how bones grow – this meets partial elements of P1.

Making bones strong

Impact exercise – running or even walking on hard ground, jumping up and down, athletic dancing – all have the effect of promoting bone growth and strengthening our bones. It's important to do this because as we get older our bones get more brittle.

Joints

Where one bone meets another is a joint. There are fixed joints (such as where the bones making up your skull have fused together), slightly moveable joints (which do what their name says – an example of this is where your ribs meet your breast bone, there is a bit of movement but it's not like ...) moveable joints like knees, hips, wrists.

These are called synovial joints. There are six types and they allow different sorts of movement.

Example of joint	Type	Example of movement
Shoulder (also hip)	Ball and socket	Rotating movements: tennis player using shoulder to generate forehand ground stroke
Wrist (also ankle)	Condyloid	Movement in 2 directions: climber finding footholds on climbing wall
Neck (also spine)	Pivot	Spectators watching a tennis match moving their heads from side to side tracking the ball
Knees (also elbows)	Hinge	Allow you to move in 1 direction only – so bending your elbow when throwing a javelin

This table shows your knowledge of the various forms of joints in the body; this with the descriptions above meets partial elements of P1.

The other two types are not as important. A saddle joint is only found in our thumbs and this joint allows us to move our thumbs backwards and forwards and side to side. We have gliding joints in our hands which allow limited movements.

Arthritis can affect our joints as we get older. At the joint surface the smooth covering is worn away leaving rough bone which causes pain as we move. But it's not only older people who get arthritis. People who have done lots of jogging on hard pavements can develop arthritis in their knees. Sports people who have had injury can develop arthritis in joints they have injured. This is why it's very important, whatever sport you are taking part in to warm up and down properly.

The skeleton for movement

> This is a good description of one of the functions of the skeletal system – this meets partial elements of P1.

It is our skeleton that allows us to move. Suppose you were going to lift weights. The biceps muscle at the front of your upper arm would contract, whilst the triceps muscle at the back would relax and stretch. This would have the effect of raising your lower arm with the weight. To lower the weight exactly the opposite would happen. The triceps contract whilst the biceps relax. This allows you to lower your lower arm. If you raise your lower arm and put your other hand on your biceps muscle you can feel it bulking out as it contracts. If you rotate the hand on your raised arm, you can feel the muscle becoming even more pronounced. When any bit of us moves at least two sets of muscles are at work – one set contracting and the opposite set relaxing.

> Margaret, you need to give the source of all your diagrams.

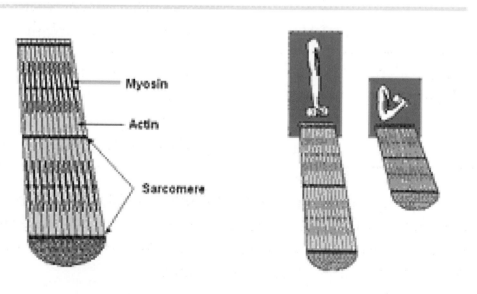

Skeletal Muscle Contraction

Myosin

Actin

Sarcomere

Ligaments and tendons

Ligaments are what hold one bone to another and tendons attach muscle to bone. These are like thick sheets of elastic and are often the things that get injured when there's a joint injury.

As a sports person it is important to look after ligaments and tendons. You must make sure they are stretched – and before exercise you should do gentle stretching exercises. This will allow you the full range of movement and prevent injury.

Sport and our bodies

If we don't do sport very often, or do a new sport, we might find that our muscles ache a bit because they have been stretched and are not used to the exercise. However, if we do something regularly, eg circuits, then our muscles stretch, as do our ligaments and tendons and we don't feel sore after a session. We become more supple and mobile. This can only be good for us.

In the long-term, our joints will also get stronger which means we are less likely to get injured in the future.

In the short term, changes can occur in the increased production of synovial fluid, which can be found around all synovial joints.

This will mean that as we do get older we will be much fitter, far less likely to suffer injury and less likely top break bones and become immobile.

> Margaret, in this section you have identified the effects of exercise on the skeletal system commenting on both long and short term effects, by doing this you have met P2 in full.

Sources of information

Textbook: BTEC First Sport by J Stafford-Brown, S Rea, L Janaway and C Manley, published by Hodder-Arnold

Websites:

www.bbc.co.uk/science/humanbody/body/factfiles/bonegrowth

www.dancesport.uk.com/shoes/conchart.htm

www.kidshealth.org/teen/your_body/body_basics/bones_muscles_joints.html

My notes made in class

Tutor feedback

Task 1 (P1, P2)
Margaret Harper

A good effort! You have described the structure, function of the skeletal system and how bones grow therefore you have achieved P1 criterion in full, however I would expect you to add the scapula to your diagram on page number 1.

You have identified (P2) the effects of exercise on bones and joints and include good use of diagrams to illustrate your understanding. Your work is well written and well presented.

To achieve M2 in this assessment you must explain both the long and short term effects of exercise on the bones and joints and expand on your identifications that you have made at the end of this assessment.

You have not attempted the distinction part of this assignment which was to analyse the effects of exercise on the musculoskeletal system. This must be attempted for you to possibly achieve this.

Achieved P1, P2 of the grading criteria

Pass/Merit level answer

Faisal Ahmed – Task 1 (P1, P2) and Task 2 (P2, M2)

A GUIDE TO THE STRUCTURE AND FUNCTION OF THE SKELETAL SYSTEM

Task 1 (P1)

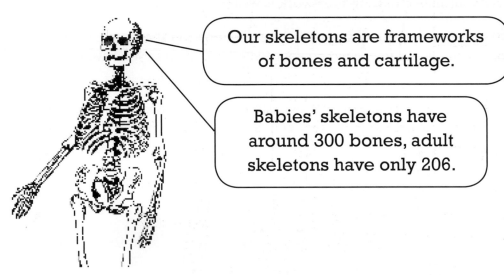

> Our skeletons are frameworks of bones and cartilage.

> Babies' skeletons have around 300 bones, adult skeletons have only 206.

Faisal, you do need to acknowledge the source of this diagram.

Skeletons perform five specific functions within the body:

- **Protection** – the skeleton provides protection for the organs it surrounds, for example the heart, lungs and brain.

  ✓

- **Shape and Support** – the skeleton provides a framework which surrounds the body.

  ✓

- **Movement** – our bones are connected to other bones at flexible joints which allow varying degrees of movement. Bones are attached to muscles by tendons and joints by ligaments. These then act as levers which move the bone as, how and when desired.

  ✓

- **To Provide a Storage Site for Inorganic Salts** – our bones store minerals such as calcium and phosphorus within them, some fats are also stored within our bones.

  ✓

- **Blood Cell Production** – red and white blood cells and platelets are manufactured and stored within our bones in the bone marrow. Red blood cells carry oxygen to our muscles and organs such as the brain and heart. White blood cells fight infections as a part of the body's immune system. Platelets are important for blood clotting.

A clear identification of the functions of the skeleton displaying basic understanding.

The Bones of the Body

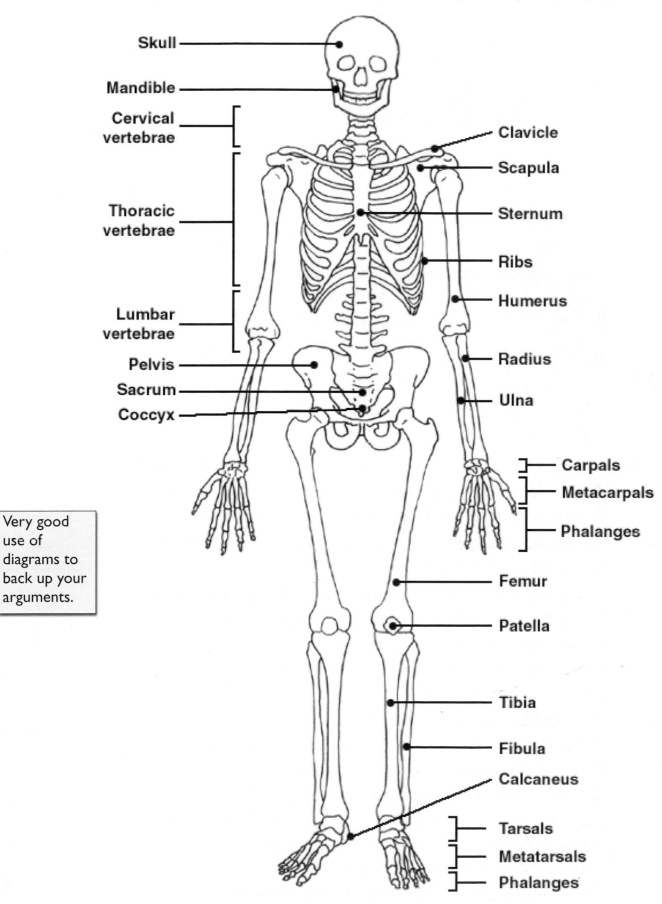

Skull

Mandible

Cervical vertebrae

Thoracic vertebrae

Lumbar vertebrae

Pelvis

Sacrum

Coccyx

Clavicle

Scapula

Sternum

Ribs

Humerus

Radius

Ulna

Carpals

Metacarpals

Phalanges

Femur

Patella

Tibia

Fibula

Calcaneus

Tarsals

Metatarsals

Phalanges

Very good use of diagrams to back up your arguments.

Fig. 1

The Major Bones of the Body

- **The Skull** – this is made up of the cranium which protects the brain and facial bones.

- **The Ribs** – these are flat bones which are joined to the sternum and form a cage around the heart and lungs.

- **The Sternum** – this is often called the breast bone and is located in the middle of the chest.

- **The Pelvis** – this protects the lower internal organs e.g. the reproductive organs and bladder.

- **The Clavicle** – this connects the upper arm to the main part of the body. ✓

- **The Scapula** – this is often called the shoulder blade, this is situated on the back of the body. ✓

- **The Arm** – this is made up of three bones: the humerus (upper arm), the radius and the ulna (lower arm). ✓

- **The Leg** – this is made up of four bones: the femur (thigh bone), the tibia (shin bone), the fibula (lower leg) and the patella (kneecap). ✓

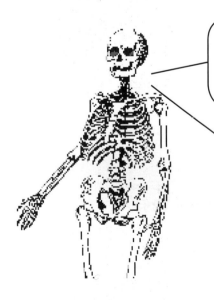

Bone is a living tissue with a blood supply; it can repair itself when broken.

When we are born, our bones are made almost entirely from cartilage.

Bone Growth

Bones are made of cartilage when we are born. As we grow, calcium (supplied through our diets) is deposited within the cartilage; the cartilage then hardens and eventually becomes bone. The calcium is pushed towards the end of the bones as new cartilage is grown in the centre of the bones. When a baby stops growing new cartilage, the entire bone has been calcified, growth is finished. This process is called Ossification and makes adult bones strong and rigid. Babies skeletons have 300 bones, adult skeletons have only 206, some of the baby's bones fuse together to form bigger bones.

Bones grow in length at either end in areas called growth plates. This growth occurs when cartilage cells divide and increase in number in these growth plates. The new cartilage cells push older, larger cartilage cells towards the middle of the bone. In time older cartilage cells die and are replaced with bone. When a bone has reached its full size, its growth plates are converted into bone.

> Faisal, this is a good explanation of the Ossification process. You explain well the transformation from cartilage to bone.

> Good diagram to back up your above explanation of bone growth.

An Illustration of Bone Growth

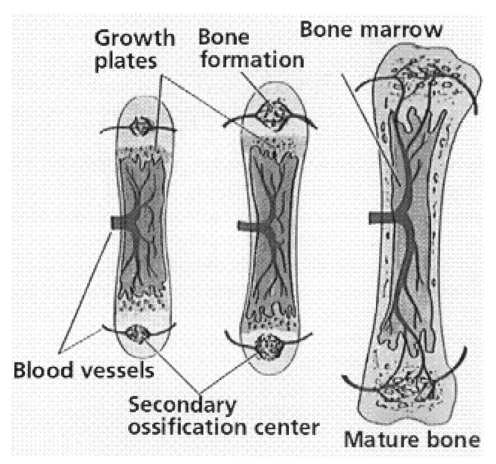

Fig.2

Task 2 (P2, M2)

The Effect of Exercise on our Bones and Joints

Exercise has a positive effect on the body as a whole, especially the skeletal system. Participating in regular weight bearing exercise results in a happier, longer and healthier life.

The Short Term Effects of Exercise:

- **Increased strength, decreased risk of injury** – when we exercise regularly the skeleton becomes stronger; it is therefore more able to withstand impact. Consequently if an injury does occur it will usually be less severe and we will therefore be quicker to recover. This is because when we exercise we increase the mineral content in our bones, which makes them harder and stronger. This effect is reversible, when we stop participating in exercise these gains in bone mass and strength will be reversed.

  ✓

- **Increased strength in joints** – when we exercise we make our joints stronger. This is because the cartilage at the end of our bones becomes thicker and the production of synovial fluid increases. We are therefore less likely to suffer from a joint injury.

  ✓
  Could you possibly have explained what a joint injury is?

- **Improved posture** – when we exercise our muscles become stronger, this helps keep the skeleton in proper alignment, reduces back and leg pain and improves our posture in general.

  ✓
  What could be the effects of bad posture?

The Long Term Effects of Exercise:

- **Reduced occurrence of Arthritis** – regular moderate exercise can prevent cartilage abnormalities such as pitting and fissuring, and therefore improves joint cartilage health i.e. decreases the occurrence of arthritis.

  ✓

- **Increased occurrence of Arthritis – high stress exercise** can cause damage and deterioration to joint cartilage, therefore increasing the chances of arthritis. If a damaged joint is not rested after injury this can also result in arthritis.

  ✓

- **Reduced occurrence of Osteoporosis (bone loss)**
  – Osteoporosis is a condition, which mostly effects middle-aged and elderly women, the bones become weak and brittle, sufferers are therefore more at risk from fractures and injuries after even minor accidents and falls. Regular exercise from an early age and throughout life increases bone mass and therefore reduces the risk of developing osteoporosis.

References:

Anatomy and Physiology for Therapists.

Connor.J, Harwwod-Pearce.V, Morgan.K,2006

BTEC First Sport, For Performance, Exercise and Fitness and Outdoor Recreation.

Stafford-Brown, J. Rea, S. Janaway, L. Manley. C, 2006

✓ **Weight Training Basics.**

Fahey.TD, 2005,

Websites:

Fig.1 www.patient.co.uk

Fig.2 www.emc.maricopa.edu

www. Britannica .com

www. BBC Science and Nature: Human Body and Mind

www. Sporting-Heroes.net

www. Sporting Performance.co.uk

www. Shelfieldpeonline.co.uk

Tutor feedback

Task 1 (P1, P2) and Task 2 (P2, M2)
Faisal Ahmed

Faisal, this is good piece of work. You have described the structure, function of the skeletal system and how bones grow therefore you have achieved P1 criterion in full.

You have identified (P2) the effects of exercise on bones and joints and include good use of diagrams to illustrate your understanding. Your work is well written and well presented.

You clearly explain (M2) both the long and short term effects of exercise on the bones and joints, however at times you could have expanded upon some of your answers.

You have not attempted the distinction part of this assignment which was to analyse the effects of exercise on the musculoskeletal system. This must be attempted for you to possibly achieve this.

Achieved P1, P2 and M2 of the grading criteria

Pass/Merit/Distinction level answer

Amy Tan – Task 1 (P1, P2), Task 2 (P2, M2) and Task 3 (D2)

Task 1
WHAT IS OUR SKELETAL SYSTEM? (P1)

A detailed diagram clearly identifying the skeletal system. However, you do need to label the scapula. Good evidence of external research.

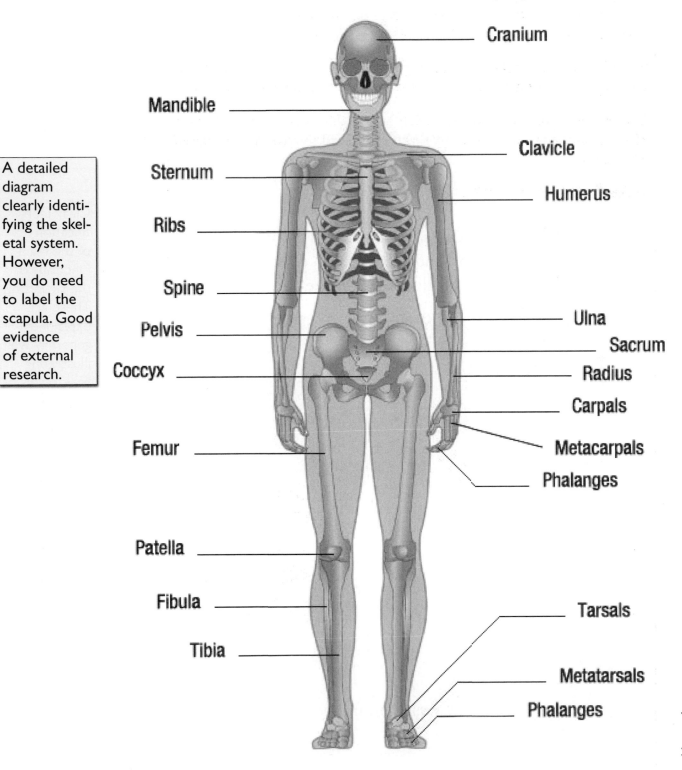

Cranium
Mandible
Sternum
Ribs
Spine
Pelvis
Coccyx
Femur
Patella
Fibula
Tibia
Clavicle
Humerus
Ulna
Sacrum
Radius
Carpals
Metacarpals
Phalanges
Tarsals
Metatarsals
Phalanges

© bbc.co.uk

✓   www.BBC Science and Nature: Human Body and Mind

The skeleton performs five main functions within the body; movement, support, protection, mineral storage and blood production.

Support – Our skeleton is an upright frame under our skin which provides support for the body and muscles, and a place for internal organs to sit.

Protection – Our skeleton protects our internal organs for example our heart and brain from damage.

Movement – Our skeletal bones are attached to muscles which pull on them and provide us with many different movements.

Mineral Storage – Minerals such as calcium and phosphorus are stored in our bones, we need these minerals to maintain the bones hardness and strength so they can function correctly. Over time these mineral levels diminish, if they are not replaced conditions such as Osteoporosis can occur. It is therefore vital that we eat a healthy diet high in minerals.

Development of Blood Cells – Some bones within our body e.g. sternum, vertebral column and pelvic girdle, contain bone marrow which is essential for the production of white and red blood cells.

WHAT ARE OUR BONES MADE FROM? (P1)

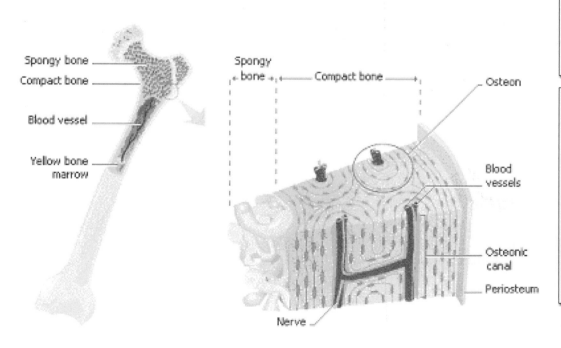

www.britannica.com

> ✓

> ✓

> ✓
> Could the 'many different movements' be identified?

> ✓
> Clear identification of the main functions of the skeleton. These are explained generally well illustrating basic levels of knowledge.

> Again very good use of diagrams to back up and emphasise major points made in your work. This improves the quality of your answers.

Our bones are made up of five different compounds:

Poriosteum – this contains nerves and blood vessels which feed the bone, it also provides a thin outer layer.

Compact bone – this is hard and strong, it provides an outer casing for the bone.

Spongy bone – this is full of small holes (like a sponge) and is found within compact bone.

Bone Marrow – this is found in the middle of certain bones e.g. the sternum, and vertebral column, and provides white and red blood cells.

Cancellous bone – this is like a honeycomb under magnification and provides protection for the bone marrow.

HOW DO OUR BONES GROW? (P1)

In the initial stages of embryo growth, within the womb, our skeletons are made from cartilage. This is slowly replaced by bone, this process is called Ossification. This continues through early childhood until nearly all our skeletons are made up of bone. Our skeleton continues to change until we are about 25 years old, by this time our final size and shape has been determined.

A correct identification of the five different bone compounds. Your work however could be presented in more detail. While the above is factually correct a greater explanation would enhance this specific part of your assignment.

TASK 2

SHORT TERM effects of exercise on our bones and joints (P2)	Explanation (M2)
Bone hardening and strengthening	Exercise results in an increase in mineral content in our bones
Stronger joints and therefore decreased risk of injury	Exercise results in an increase in the thickness of our cartilage at the ends of the bones and an increase in the production of synovial fluid. This therefore results in stronger joints.
Better skeletal alignment and prevention of back and leg pain.	Increased muscle strength helps provide the support necessary for good posture, and can therefore minimise stresses to the back and legs.
Increased strength in tendons	We are therefore at a lower risk of injury from damage to these tissues.

How will this affect our bones?

What will be the benefits of this?

Bad posture therefore will result in?

What sort of sporting injuries are we less at risk from?

LONG TERM effects of exercise on our bones and joints (P2)	Explanation (M2)
Prevention or delay of Osteoporosis (bone loss)	Bones respond to stress and disuse by reducing tissue in areas where it is no longer needed and increasing it in areas that are subjected to stress. Exercise causes bone growth, inactivity causes bone loss and therefore Osteoporosis.
Prevention or delay of Sarcopenia (muscle loss)	After the age of 30 people begin to lose muscle mass and strength, also motor nerves become disconnected from the portion of muscle they control. Exercise helps to maintain motor nerve connections and therefore the speed and effectiveness of our muscles.
Prevention and cause of Arthritis	Moderate regular exercise can prevent early cartilage degeneration and maintain normal joint cartilage; this may therefore decrease the risk of developing arthritis. Conversely to this, the risk of developing arthritis may also increase when people take part in *high* impact sports (football, weight lifting) as it can also *cause* cartilage degeneration.

A good clear explanation.

Good understanding shown.

A good link between theory and practice. Well done, Amy.

✓

Task 3
WHAT EFFECT DOES EXERCISE HAVE ON OUR BONES AND JOINTS? (D2)

There are many reasons why it is beneficial to participate in sporting activities, one of the most significant being the effects it has on the bones and joints within our bodies.

In general, if we take part in exercise on a regular basis our skeletons will become stronger and more able to withstand impact i.e. we are less likely to suffer from injuries, if they do occur we are able to recover more quickly.

AN ANALYSIS OF THE EFFECTS OF EXERCISE ON THE MUSCULOSKELETAL SYSTEM (D2)

The musculoskeletal system involves the skeletal system and the muscular system working in co-operation with each other, in this instance during exercise.

When we participate in regular weight-bearing exercise (weight bearing exercise is where we are using our body weight as a form of resistance e.g. running or walking) we exert stress on our muscles and bones we would not normally do in everyday life. If this is controlled and the level built up gradually then this has a very beneficial effect on the musculoskeletal system. Muscles become larger, stronger, less likely to tire or become injured and muscle loss which occurs with age (sarcopenia) is reduced. Our bones also become stronger, less likely to fracture and less likely to suffer from degenerative conditions such as osteoporosis and arthritis.

If our musculoskeletal systems are subjected to too much stress, or are over used, injury may occur for example a shin splint or muscle strain. If there are any signs or symptoms of injury these must be detected and dealt with and the musculoskeletal system rested before exercise is recommended to avoid further complications.

In conclusion if exercise is performed regularly and gradually increased both in length of time spent training and the resistance level or speed, then exercise has a very positive effect on the musculoskeletal system which will allow a happier, injury free and longer life.

> ✓
> Why are we able to recover from injury more easily and quickly? Try to substantiate and back up your arguments with specific examples.

> A good analysis highlighting the benefits and negatives of an efficient skeletal and muscular system.
> ✓

Tutor feedback

Task 1 (P1, P2), Task 2 (P2, M2) and Task 3 (D2)
Amy Tan

Amy, you have produced an assignment that shows good understanding of the set tasks. All questions are answered well, covering the unit content, and using good English.

You have described the structure, function of the skeletal system and how bones grow therefore **you have achieved P1 criterion in full**.

You successfully identify (P2) the effects of exercise on bones and joints with good use of diagrams to emphasise your main points. You also explain (M2) the effects of exercise on bones and joints well in the form of a table. Your analysis (D2) again highlights subject knowledge and you present a well-written argument.

A very good piece of work successfully achieving all of the (P2, M2, D2) available criteria. Well done!